my SISTER, *my* BROTHER

LIFE TOGETHER IN CHRIST

Henri J. M. Nouwen

A Compilation by
The Word Among Us Press

D0179665

the WORD
among us®
Press

The Word Among Us Press
9639 Doctor Perry Road
Ijamsville, Maryland 21754
www.wordamongus.org

ISBN: 1-59325-065-7
09 08 07 06   2 3 4 5

Additional acknowledgments begin on p. 141.
Learn more about Nouwen, his writing, and the work of the Henri Nouwen Society at www.HenriNouwen.org.

Made and printed in the United States of America

Library of Congress Cataloging-in-Publication Data

Nouwen, Henri J. M.
   My sister, my brother : life together in Christ / Henri J. M. Nouwen.-- 1st American pbk. ed.
      p. cm.
   Includes bibliographical references.
   ISBN 1-59325-065-7 (alk. paper)
   1. Church. 2. Fellowship--Religious aspects--Christianity. 3. Catholic Church--Doctrines. I. Title. BX1746.N68 2005
   262--dc22
                                        2005026872

Contents

Introduction

Communion makes us look at each other and speak to each other, not about the latest news, but about him who walked with us. We discover each other as people who belong together because each of us now belongs to him.

Henri Nouwen, *With Burning Hearts*

The mystery of Immanuel—God with us—is that we are now one in Christ. We are sons and daughters of our Father and brothers and sisters to Christ and one another. We have become the people of God, and we are joined together with the same bonds of love that join us to Christ.

Henri J. M. Nouwen was deeply aware of this mystery. His experience of living among his brothers and sisters and caring for them led him into a deeper experience of the presence of God, both in himself and in the world. He recognized the imperative to live a common life, to support, affirm, and encourage one another because we are "people who together make God visible in the world" (*Can You Drink the Cup?*).

My Sister, My Brother: Life Together in Christ features selections from Nouwen's many writings—some forty books—that address some aspect of this communion to which we are called. The readings are presented topically, starting with God's desire for us to live in the love of the Trinity. Other sections address the mystery of the Eucharist in bringing us together, the disciplines necessary to live together in Christ, the need to pray with and for others, the strength and gifts we discover in one another, and the bonds we share with the saints who have gone before us. All eight sections include at least one prayer, drawing the topic to the heart of God, the foundation of our life together.

Since the 1970s the writings of Henri Nouwen have touched a responsive chord in the hearts of men and women who longed for a deeper relationship with God and his people. Nouwen was a priest who had extensive training in psychology, and he was able to bridge the two worlds of theology and social science. However, his work also resonated on a more personal level. Though deeply devout, he was restless in spirit. It often seems as if his writings were as much for himself as for his readers. And that is what makes them so powerful.

Because the selections are not presented in the order they were written, the scenes often change from page to page, alternating among several time frames and settings. In the 1970s Nouwen was by and large in an Ivy League setting, teaching pastoral theology to divinity students. In 1974 he took his first of several sabbaticals, living with the Trappists at Genesee Abbey in western New York; in this setting Nouwen wrote the first of several published diaries, which feature a chronicling voice. In the early eighties, he spent six months in Peru and Bolivia, in language school and living among the poor. After returning to a New England classroom for a few years, in 1985 he embarked on a new life with the L'Arche communities, in which able-bodied adults live with and assist adults with severe disabilities. For ten years he was pastor of the L'Arche Daybreak community near Toronto. In September 1996, while visiting his homeland of Holland, Henri suffered a massive heart attack and died, just months before his sixty-fifth birthday.

Although Henri Nouwen is no longer writing, his insightful and moving body of work continues to inspire Christians of all denominations. In life Henri boldly claimed the Triune God as his true home. In faith we pray God's rest for him, in the eternal home prepared for him by his Lord, within the community of heaven.

We want to thank the editorial team responsible for putting together this compilation, particularly Evelyn Bence for her careful and thoughtful research. We pray that this book will inspire you to reach out to your brothers and sisters in Christ to live together in a way that makes God visible in the world today.

The Word Among Us Press

PART I

TOGETHER IN
THE HEART OF GOD

God Is the Hub

Last night, this morning, and this afternoon I was part of a retreat of twenty-five students from the Newman Center of Geneseo State College. It is the first time since May that I have given conferences or meditations. I used a large wagon wheel to make the point that the closer we come to God—the hub of our life—the closer we come to each other, even when we travel along very different paths (spokes). The wheel stayed in the center of the room during the retreat. . . .

God is the hub of the wheel of life. The closer we come to God the closer we come to each other. The basis of community is not primarily our ideas, feelings, and emotions about each other but our common search for God. When we keep our minds and hearts directed toward God, we will come more fully "together." During my stay in the Abbey I saw and experienced how many men with very different backgrounds and characters can live together in peace. They can do so not because of mutual attraction toward each other, but because of the common attraction toward God, their Lord and Father.

The Genesee Diary

The Trinity as Our Home

Trinity Sunday. Beautiful weather. Sunny, cool, no wind, many birds chirping, very quiet. Peggy suggested that we celebrate the Eucharist in Mimi's garden, created in memory of her deceased daughter.

About twenty people sat in a large circle in the lovely fenced-in garden. I tried to explain the mystery of the Trinity by saying that all human relationships are reflections of the relationships within God. God is the Lover, the Beloved, the Love that binds us in unity. God invites us to be part of that inner movement of love so that we can truly become sons and daughters of the Father, sisters and brothers of the Son, and spouses of the Holy Spirit. Thus, all our human relationships can be lived *in* God, and as witness to God's divine presence in our lives.

I am deeply convinced that most human suffering comes from broken relationships. Anger, jealousy, resentment, and feelings of rejection all find their source in conflict between people who yearn for unity, community, and a deep sense of belonging. By claiming the Holy Trinity as home for our relational lives, we claim the truth that God gives us what we most desire and offers us the grace to forgive each other for not being perfect in love. We had a good discussion about this mystery of love and a joyful celebration of the Eucharist.

Sabbatical Journey

Rest in the Divine Covenant

Bonds that last cannot be based simply on good, better, or excellent interpersonal relationships but must be rooted outside the many devices and desires of the wounded human heart. Rooted in a bond that existed before and beyond human togetherness, bonds of true intimacy rest in the divine covenant. This is the covenant of God's faithfulness expressed in the promises made to Noah, Abraham and Sarah, Moses and the prophets, and made fully visible in the incarnation of Jesus.

God alone is free enough from wounds to offer us a fearless space. In and through God we can be faithful to each other: in friendship, marriage, and community. This intimate bond with God, constantly nurtured by prayer, offers us a true home. We can live together in this home without asking for much more than a willingness to constantly confess our weaknesses to each other and to always forgive each other. Jean Vanier considers this divine covenant the basis of every form of human faithfulness. We can only stay together when the "staying power" comes from the One who comes to us to stay. When we know ourselves to be deeply anchored in that divine covenant, we can build homes together. Only then can our limited and broken love reflect the unlimited and unbroken love of God.

Lifesigns

God's Faithful Presence as Home

During the Eucharist this morning we talked about God's covenant. God says, "I am your God and will be faithful to you even when you won't be faithful to me." Through human history, this divine faithfulness is shown to us in God's increasing desire for intimacy. At first God was the God *for* us, our protector and shield. Then, when Jesus came, God became the God *with* us, our companion and friend. Finally, when Jesus sent his Spirit, God was revealed to us as the God *within* us, our very breath and heartbeat.

Our life is full of brokenness—broken relationships, broken promises, broken expectations. How can we live that brokenness without becoming bitter and resentful except by returning again and again to God's faithful presence in our lives? Without this "place" of return, our journey easily leads us to darkness and despair. But with this safe and solid home, we can keep renewing our faith, and keep trusting that the many setbacks of life move us forward to an always greater bond with the God of the covenant.

Sabbatical Journey

The Spirit Is Love Itself

This inexhaustible love between the Father and the Son includes and yet transcends all forms of love known to us. It includes the love of a father and mother, a brother and sister, a husband and wife, a teacher and friend. But it also goes far beyond the many limited and limiting human experiences of love we know. It is a caring yet demanding love. It is a supportive yet severe love. It is a gentle yet strong love. It is a love that gives life yet accepts death. In this divine love Jesus was sent into the world, to this divine love Jesus offered himself on the cross. This all-embracing love, which epitomizes the relationship between the Father and the Son, is a divine Person, coequal with the Father and the Son. It has a personal name. It is called the Holy Spirit. The Father loves the Son and pours himself out in the Son. The Son is loved by the Father and returns all he is to the Father. The Spirit is love itself, eternally embracing the Father and the Son.

Making All Things New

The Likeness of the Divine Life

Leonid Ouspensky tells us that two icons are especially venerated in Russian churches on the day of Pentecost: the icon of the Descent of the Holy Spirit and the icon of the Holy Trinity. Thus, the intimate connection between the birth of the community of faith and the mystery of the Triune God is expressed. . . .

This trinitarian vision of the church helps us comprehend the full meaning of brotherly and sisterly love. Jesus had already told his disciples that his love for them was as full as the love of his Father for him, and that their love for each other should be as full as the love of Jesus for them . . . (see John 15:9, 12). At Pentecost he sends them the Holy Spirit, the spirit of love with which the Father and Son love each other, thus creating a community according to the likeness of the divine life. Just as Adam and Eve were created in the image of God, so the church was created in the image of the triune life of God revealed by Jesus the Christ. Therefore, it is significant that Jesus' words, "Love one another as I have loved you" (John 15:12, NRSV) are directed to his most intimate friends, his disciples. Those who know Jesus are called to manifest his love in their common life, and thus become a sign of hope in the midst of a fearful world.

Behold the Beauty of the Lord

Baptized into a New Community

[Jesus,] I look at your pierced side, and I see not only blood coming out, but water as well. . . . The water that flows from your side is a life-giving water. Not only is it a water that cleanses me from sin, but it is also water that brings me into a new land, a new home, a new community. It is the water of the Red Sea through which your people were led out of Egypt. It is the water that gushed forth from the rock in the desert to quench your people's thirst. It is the water from the Jordan through which the people and the Ark of the Covenant passed to enter into the promised land. It is the water that flowed from the Temple, becoming deeper and deeper. It is the water with which you yourself were baptized by John. It is the water that became wine at Cana. It is the healing water of the pool of Bethesda. It is the water with which you washed your disciples' feet.

Yes, Lord, the water flowing from your side is all of this, but much more than this too because it is the water by which you give us your innermost self and make us part of your communion with your Father; it is water that becomes a spring in us welling up for eternal life. Yes, Lord, the water flowing from your broken heart makes me into a new person, a child of your Father, and your brother. It is the water of baptism that has been poured over me and so many others and that has given entrance to the new community fashioned by your Spirit.

Heart Speaks to Heart

Community: First and Foremost a Gift

Community is first and foremost a gift of the Holy Spirit, not built upon mutual compatibility, shared affection or common interests, but upon having received the same divine breath, having been given a heart set aflame by the same divine fire and having been embraced by the same divine love. It is the God-within who brings us into communion with each other and makes us one. This message both confronts and consoles us. It confronts us with our inability to heal our own brokenness with self-made solutions, and it consoles us with the revelation that God indeed does want to create among us the unity we most long for.

Behold the Beauty of the Lord

Like a Large Mosaic

Community is like a large mosaic. Each little piece seems so insignificant. One piece is bright red, another cold blue or dull green, another warm purple, another sharp yellow, another shining gold. Some look precious, others ordinary. Some look valuable, others worthless. Some look gaudy, others delicate. As individual stones, we can do little with them except compare them and judge their beauty and value. When, however, all these little stones are brought together in one big mosaic portraying the face of Christ, who would ever question the importance of any one of them? If one of them, even the least spectacular one, is missing, the face is incomplete. Together in the one mosaic, each little stone is indispensable and makes a unique contribution to the glory of God. That's community, a fellowship of little people who together make God visible in the world.

Can You Drink the Cup?

Rest in the Embrace of God

The word that seems best to summarize the desire of the human heart is "communion." Communion means "union with." God has given us a heart that will remain restless until it has found full communion. We look for it in friendship, in marriage, in community. We look for it in sexual intimacy, in moments of ecstasy, in the recognition of our gifts. We look for it through success, admiration, and rewards. But wherever we look, it is communion that we seek.

As I looked at the faces of the gold medalists at the Olympics, with more than sixty thousand people applauding them and millions watching them on television, I caught a glimpse of that momentary experience of communion. It seemed as if they had, finally, received the love they had worked for with unwavering dedication. And still, how soon they will be forgotten. . . .

Still, the desire for communion remains. It is a God-given desire, a desire that causes immense pain as well as immense joy. Jesus came to proclaim that our desire for communion is not in vain, but will be fulfilled by the One who gave us that desire. The passing moments of communion are only hints of the Communion that God has promised us. The real danger facing us is to distrust our desire for communion. It is a God-given desire without which our lives lose their vitality and our hearts grow cold. A truly spiritual life is life in which we won't rest until we have found rest in the embrace of the One who is the Father and Mother of all desires.

Here and Now

God's Ongoing Incarnation

For over a year Nouwen served as the morning assistant to Adam, a young man with severe disabilities at the L'Arche Daybreak community.

My friend had a lot more questions about Adam and the people who lived with me in my home: "Why spend so much time and money on people with severe disabilities while so many capable people can hardly survive?" And, "Why should such people be allowed to take time and energy which should be given to solving the real problems humanity is facing?"

I didn't answer my friend's questions. I didn't argue or discuss his "issues." I felt deeply that I had nothing very intelligent to say that would change my friend's mind. My daily two hours with Adam were transforming me. In being present to him I was hearing an inner voice of love beyond all the activities of care. Those two hours were pure gift, a time of contemplation, during which we, together, were touching something of God. With Adam I knew a sacred presence and I "saw" the face of God.

For many years I had reserved the word "Incarnation" for the historic event of God's coming to us in Jesus. Being so close with Adam I realized that the "Christ event" is much more than something that took place long ago. It occurs every time spirit greets spirit in the body. It is a sacred event happening in the present because it is God's event among people. That is what the sacramental life is all about. It is God's ongoing incarnation whenever people meet each other "in God's name."

Adam

God Asks for a Single-Minded Commitment

Jesus' primary concern was to be obedient to his Father, to live constantly in his presence. Only then did it become clear to him what his task was in his relationships with people. This also is the way he proposes for his apostles: "It is to the glory of my Father that you should bear much fruit and be my disciples" (John 15:8, JB). Perhaps we must continually remind ourselves that the first commandment requiring us to love God with all our heart, all our soul, and all our mind is indeed the first. I wonder if we really believe this. It seems that in fact we live as if we should give as much of our heart, soul, and mind as possible to our fellow human beings, while trying hard not to forget God. At least we feel that our attention should be divided evenly between God and our neighbor. But Jesus' claim is much more radical. He asks for a single-minded commitment to God and God alone. God wants all of our heart, all of our mind, and all of our soul. It is this unconditional and unreserved love for God that leads to the care for our neighbor, not as an activity which distracts us from God or competes with our attention to God, but as an expression of our love for God who reveals himself to us as the God of all people. It is in God that we find our neighbors and discover our responsibility to them. We might even say that only in God does our neighbor become a neighbor rather than an infringement upon our autonomy, and that only in and through God does service become possible.

The Living Reminder

Give All Your Love to Me

This morning during the Eucharist we discussed the great commandment. . . . When we love God with all our heart, mind, strength, and soul, we cannot do other than love our neighbor, and our very selves. It is by being fully rooted in the heart of God that we are creatively connected with our neighbor as well as with our deepest self. In the heart of God we can see that the other human beings who live on this earth with us are also God's sons and daughters, and belong to the same family we do. There too I can recognize and claim my own belovedness, and celebrate it with my neighbors.

Our society thinks economically: "How much love do I give to God, how much to my neighbor, and how much to myself?" But God says, "Give all your love to me, and I will give you your neighbor and yourself."

We are not talking here about moral obligations or ethical imperatives. We are talking about the mystical life. It is the intimate communion with God that reveals to us how to live in the world and act in God's Name.

Sabbatical Journey

The Second Commandment

The first commandment receives concreteness and specificity through the second; the second commandment becomes possible through the first. The first and second commandments should never be separated or made mutually exclusive, neither should they be confused or substituted one for the other. That is why the second commandment is equal to the first, and that is why all ministry is based on our personal and communal relationship with God. This is what Dietrich Bonhoeffer says in his books, *The Communion of Saints* and *The Cost of Discipleship*. It is also the core idea of Thomas Merton's writings, and it was the intuition of all the great Christian leaders, who considered a growing intimacy with Christ the source of all their actions.

And so, to be living reminders of God we must be concerned first of all with our own intimacy with God. Once we have heard, seen, watched, and touched the Word who is life, we cannot do other than be living reminders. Once our lives are connected with his, we will speak about him, sing his praise, and proclaim his great deeds, not out of obligation but as a free, spontaneous response. In order for this response to be lasting and oriented to the felt needs of those to whom we minister, we need discipline, formation, and training. But these can do little more than offer channels for the lived experience of God.

The Living Reminder

PART 2

COMMUNION CREATES COMMUNITY

God Desires Communion

The word that best expresses this mystery of God's total self-giving love is "communion." It is the word that contains the truth that, in and through Jesus, God wants, not only to teach us, instruct us, or inspire us, but to become one with us. God desires to be fully united with us so that all of God and all of us can be bound together in a lasting love. The whole long history of God's relationship with us human beings is a history of ever-deepening communion. It is not simply a history of unities, separations, and restored unities, but a history in which God searches for ever-new ways to commune intimately with those created in God's own image. . . .

God desires communion: a unity that is vital and alive, an intimacy that comes from both sides, a bond that is truly mutual. Nothing forced or "willed," but a communion freely offered and received. God goes all the way to make this communion possible. God becomes a child dependent on human care, a boy in need of guidance, a teacher searching for students, a prophet crying for followers, and, finally, a dead man pierced by a soldier's lance and laid in a tomb. At the very end of the story, he stands there looking at us, asking with eyes full of tender expectation: "Do you love me?" . . .

It is this intense desire of God to enter into the most intimate relationship with us that forms the core of the Eucharistic celebration and the Eucharistic life. God not only wants to enter human history by becoming a person who lives in a specific epoch and a specific country, but God wants to become our daily food and drink at any time and any place.

With Burning Hearts

The Emmaus Story:
Communion Creates Community

Communion with Jesus means becoming like him. With him we are nailed on the cross, with him we are laid in the tomb, with him we are raised up to accompany lost travelers on their journey. . . . Suddenly the two disciples, who ate the bread and recognized [Jesus] are alone again. But not with the aloneness with which they began their journey. They are alone, together, and know that a new bond has been created between them. They no longer look at the ground with downcast faces. They look at each other and say: "Did our hearts not burn when he talked to us on the road and explained the Scriptures to us?"

Communion creates community. Christ, living in them, brought them together in a new way. The Spirit of the risen Christ, which entered them through the eating of the bread and drinking of the cup, not only made them recognize Christ himself but also each other as members of a new community of faith. Communion makes us look at each other and speak to each other, not about the latest news, but about him who walked with us. We discover each other as people who belong together because each of us now belongs to him. We are alone, because he disappeared from our sight, but we are together because each of us is in communion with him and so has become one body through him.

With Burning Hearts

The Eucharist Creates Community

For many years I thought that the Eucharist was first of all a celebrative expression of an already existing community. Although this is true, my recent experience has shown me that the Eucharist creates community as well as expresses it.

I started a daily Eucharist at two universities with one or two students. Gradually more came, people who did not know each other, and had very different ideas or viewpoints in religious matters, and were quite different in age, nationality, and lifestyle. Most of these people would never have chosen each other as friends or companions. But they all, often for quite different reasons, felt attracted to a daily Eucharistic celebration, in which the Word of God was proclaimed and the Body and Blood of Christ shared. Over the months these quite different people found themselves drawn by Word and Sacrament into a deep community. They discovered a bond based not on physical or emotional attractiveness, social compatibility or common interests, but on the presence of the living Christ among them. Confessing their sins together, accepting together God's mercy, listening to the Holy Scriptures together, and eating and drinking together from the same bread and cup had molded them into a new community of love.

All of them started to experience support from each other in their daily struggles, many became good friends, and some even found their partners for life. Such were the remarkable fruits of spiritual community. I saw a concrete fulfillment of Jesus' promise: "When I am lifted up from the earth, I will draw all people to myself" (John 12:32, JB).

Lifesigns

Heart Speaks to Heart

I still remember Mother Teresa once saying to me that you can't see Jesus in the poor unless you can see him in the Eucharist. At the time, that remark seemed to me a bit high-flying and pious, but now that I've spent a year living with handicapped people, I'm beginning to understand better what she meant. It isn't really possible to see Jesus in human beings if you can't see him in the hidden reality of the bread that comes down from heaven. In human beings you can see this, that, and the other: angels and devils, saints and brutes, benevolent souls and malevolent power-maniacs. However, it's only when you've learned from personal experience how much Jesus cares for you and how much he desires to be your daily food, that you can learn to see that every human heart is a dwelling place for Jesus. When your heart is touched by the presence of Jesus in the Eucharist, then you will receive new eyes capable of recognizing that same presence in the hearts of others. Heart speaks to heart. Jesus in our heart speaks to Jesus in the hearts of our fellow men and women. That's the Eucharistic mystery of which we are a part.

We want to see results, and preferably instantly. But God works in secret and with a divine patience. By taking part in the Eucharist you can come gradually to understand this. Then your heart can begin to open up to the God who suffers in the people around you.

Letters to Marc about Jesus

Aspects of Communal Worship

I still want to tell you something else concerning Luke's Emmaus story, something which has quite concrete consequences for your day-to-day life, something that will bring the event a bit closer to you.

The story was written when the first Christian congregations had already been formed. So it speaks to us not only about Jesus and the spiritual life, but also about life in the very early church. In fact, it was written within the context of a believing community and its lived experience. That gives the story a whole new dimension. It tells us something about the different aspects of communal worship: owning up to our confusion, depression, despair, and guilt; listening with an open heart to the Word of God; gathering around the table to break the bread and so to acknowledge the presence of Jesus; and going out again into the world to make known to others what we have learned and experienced. You've probably seen already that these are the various components of a Eucharistic celebration. It's there that you find confession of sin, proclamation and exposition of the Word, partaking of the Lord's Supper, and being sent out into the world. Thus you can say that each time you celebrate the Eucharist you once again make the journey from Jerusalem to Emmaus and back. You can say, too, that each time you celebrate the Eucharist you are able to achieve a bit more spiritual freedom. Freedom from the subjugating powers of this world, powers that forever try to entice you to become rich and popular, and freedom to love friend and foe.

Letters to Marc about Jesus

Listening to the Church

Listen to the church. I know that isn't a popular bit of advice at a time and in a country where the church is often seen more as an obstacle in the way than as the way to Jesus. Nevertheless, I'm deeply convinced that the greatest spiritual danger for our times is the separation of Jesus from the church. The church is the body of the Lord. Without Jesus there can be no church; and without the church we cannot stay united with Jesus. I've yet to meet anyone who has come closer to Jesus by forsaking the church. To listen to the church is to listen to the Lord of the church. Specifically, this entails taking part in the church's liturgical life. Advent, Christmas, Lent, Easter, Ascension, and Pentecost: these seasons and feasts teach you to know Jesus better and better and unite you more and more intimately with the divine life he offers you in the church.

The Eucharist is the heart of the church's life. It's there that you hear the life-giving gospel and receive the gifts that sustain that life within you. The best assurance that you'll go on listening to the church is your regular participation in the Eucharist.

Letters to Marc about Jesus

The Church as the Living Christ

When we have been wounded by the church, our temptation is to reject it. But when we reject the church it becomes very hard for us to keep touch with the living Christ. When we say, "I love Jesus, but I hate the church," we end up losing not only the church but Jesus too. The challenge is to forgive the church. This challenge is especially great because the church seldom asks us for forgiveness, at least not officially. But the church as an often fallible human organization needs our forgiveness, while the church as the living Christ among us continues to offer us forgiveness.

It is important to think about the church not as "over there" but as a community of struggling, weak people of whom we are part and in whom we meet our Lord and Redeemer.

Bread for the Journey

The Keys of the Kingdom

When you can say to Jesus, "You are the Messiah, the Son of the living God," Jesus can say to you, "You are the rock on whom I will build my church." There is a mutuality of recognition and a mutuality of truth here. When we acknowledge that God has come among us through the Messiah—his anointed One—to free us from our captivity, God can point to our solid core and make us the foundation for a community of faith.

Our "rock" quality will be revealed to us when we confess our need for salvation and healing. We can become community builders when we are humble enough to see our dependence on God.

It is sad that the dialogue between Jesus and Simon Peter has, in my church, been almost exclusively used to explain the role of the papacy. By doing so, it seems to me that we miss seeing that this exchange is for all of us. We all have to confess our need for salvation, and we all have to accept our solid center.

And the keys of the kingdom? They too belong first to all who confess Jesus as their Christ and thus come to belong to a community of faith in which our binding and unbinding happen in the Name of God. When indeed the body of Christ, formed by believers, makes decisions about its members, these are kingdom decisions. That is what Jesus refers to when he says, "Whatever you bind on earth will be bound in heaven, and whatever you loose on earth will be loosed in heaven" (Matthew 16:19, NRSV).

. . . More than ever it is important to realize that the church is not simply "over there," where the bishops are or where the pope is, but "right here," where we are around the table of the Lord.

Sabbatical Journey

A Healing Community around the Table of Christ

The heart of this day was a Eucharistic celebration in which about twenty of my Cambridge friends participated. . . . We are friends of Jesus not in a sentimental fashion, but as participants in the divine life. If we dare to claim boldly that friendship, then we can also trust in the lasting bond among each other. This mutual friendship is the splendid fruit of our kinship with Jesus. It is much more than an idea. Rather, this friendship is a tangible reality.

Many friends had asked my associate, Peter, if they could come for a short visit; Peter suggested that they all come for a Eucharistic celebration, and then lunch. I am convinced that everyone received more than I would have ever been able to give in individual encounters. What I was able to give was the friendship of Jesus expressed in the gifts of bread and wine. At the same time, people from the most different age groups, educational backgrounds, lifestyles, and characters could be together in harmony and peace and discover that their differences actually reveal their deep unity in Christ.

I have been increasingly struck by the fact that the main source of suffering of the people in a city such as Cambridge seems to lie in a sense of disconnectedness, separation, and alienation. Why should I talk with each of them individually about their pain if together they can become a healing community around the table of Christ? It was a joyful time in which prayer, songs, and sharing stories revealed the faithful presence of Jesus.

The Road to Daybreak

The Ministry of Absence

In the celebration of the sacraments, we need to be aware of the importance of a ministry of absence. This is very central in the Eucharist. What do we do there? We eat bread, but not enough to take our hunger away; we drink wine, but not enough to take our thirst away; we read from a book, but not enough to take our ignorance away. Around these "poor signs" we come together and celebrate. What then do we celebrate? The simple signs, which cannot satisfy all our desires, speak first of all of God's absence. He has not yet returned; we are still on the road, still waiting, still hoping, still expecting, still longing. We gather around the table with bread, wine, and a book to remind each other of the promise we have received and so to encourage each other to keep waiting in expectation for his return. But even as we affirm his absence we realize that he already is with us. We say to each other: "Eat and drink, this is his body and blood. The One we are waiting for is our food and drink and is more present to us than we can be to ourselves. He sustains us on the road, he nurtures us as he nurtured his people in the desert." Thus, while remembering his promises in his absence we discover and celebrate his presence in our midst.

The Living Reminder

The Balance between Closeness and Distance

The balance between closeness and distance seems to be essential for the maturation of the Christian. A good liturgy is a liturgy with full participation without a pressure to participate, a liturgy with free expression and dialogue without an urge to be too personal, a liturgy where man is free to move in closer or to take more distance without feeling that he is offending people, and a liturgy where physical contact is real but does not break through the symbolic boundaries. I don't think there will ever be a single good liturgy. The personality of the minister, the nature of the students, and the climate of the place ask for many different forms. But much more important than the particular format, canon, language, or gesture is the careful balance between closeness and distance which allows the Christian community to be intimate *and* open, to be personal *and* hospitable, to receive the daily core-group as well as the occasional visitors, to be nurturing as well as apostolic.

The problem of intimacy is very often experienced as the core problem of the emotional life of the young adult. His relationships with female as well as male friends often can be clouded by painful anxieties. Closeness is desirable as well as fearful, and it asks for a careful guide to find a vital balance which can lead to a life in which one can be committed and open-minded at the same time.

Intimacy

The Feast of Corpus Christi: Faith in Christ's Presence

Dear Lord, on this day dedicated to the Eucharist, I think of the thousands of people suffering from lack of food and of the millions suffering from lack of love. While I am well fed and well cared for, while I am enjoying the fruits of the earth and the love of the brothers, I am aware of the physical and emotional destitution of so many of my fellow human beings.

Isn't my faith in your presence in the breaking of the bread meant to reach out beyond the small circle of my brothers to the larger circle of humanity and to alleviate suffering as much as possible?

If I can recognize you in the Sacrament of the Eucharist, I must also be able to recognize you in the many hungry men, women, and children. If I cannot translate my faith in your presence under the appearance of bread and wine into action for the world, I am still an unbeliever.

I pray therefore, Lord, deepen my faith in your Eucharistic presence and help me find ways to let this faith bear fruit in the lives of many. Amen.

A Cry for Mercy

From Communion to Community to Ministry

Forming a community with family and friends, building a body of love, shaping a new people of the resurrection: all of this is not just so that we can live a life protected from the dark forces that dominate our world; it is, rather, to enable us to proclaim together to all people, young and old, white and black, poor and rich, that death does not have the last word, that hope is real and God is alive.

The Eucharist is always mission. The Eucharist that has freed us from our paralyzing sense of loss and revealed to us that the Spirit of Jesus lives within us empowers us to go out into the world and to bring good news to the poor, sight to the blind, liberty to the captives, and to proclaim that God has shown again his favor to all people. But we are not sent out alone; we are sent with our brothers and sisters who also know that Jesus lives within them.

The movement flowing from the Eucharist is the movement from communion to community to ministry. Our experience of communion first sends us to our brothers and sisters to share with them our stories and build with them a body of love. Then, as community, we can move in all directions and reach out to all people.

I am deeply aware of my own tendency to want to go from communion to ministry without forming community.

With Burning Hearts

We Become the Body of Christ

During the Eucharist we had a very lively discussion about the gospel of the multiplication of bread. What we give away multiplies, and what we hoard becomes less. One of the participants was especially intrigued with the thought that the multiplication of bread might in fact have been the result of people's willingness to share the little they had with their neighbors. The true miracle might have been not that Jesus made many loaves out of a few but that he called people to not cling to their own food but trust that there was enough for everyone. If this generosity would be practiced universally in our world, there would not be so many starving people. But this is also the Eucharistic vision: Jesus shares his Body and Blood so that we all can become a living Christ in the world. Jesus himself multiplies through giving himself away. We become the body of Christ, individually as well as communally.

Sabbatical Journey

Invisible Bonds of Love

Today is the feast of the Eucharist. . . . Certainly a special Sunday for the Eucharist never appealed to me. It was with this sort of rebellious mind that I went to listen to John Eudes. But what he said really took me away from these types of preoccupations and opened new horizons.

The Lord is at the center of all things and yet in such a quiet, unobtrusive, elusive way. He lives with us, even physically, but not in the same physical way that other elements are present to us. This transcendent physical presence is what characterizes the Eucharist. It is already the other world present in this one. In the celebration of the Eucharist we are given an enclave in our world of space and time. God in Christ is really here, and yet his physical presence is not characterized by the same limitations of space and time that we know.

The Eucharist can be seen only by those who already love the Lord and believe in his active, loving presence to us. But is that not true of every good relationship that we have? Friendship is like that, human love is like that. The bonds that unite us with those we love are invisible bonds. They become visible only indirectly, only by what we do as a result of them. But the bonds themselves are invisible. The presence of friends to one another is very real; this presence is palpably physical, sustaining us in difficult or joyful moments and yet invisible.

The Genesee Diary

The Church, God's People

As Jesus was one human person among many, the church is one organization among many. And just as there may have been people with more attractive appearances than Jesus, there may be many organizations that are a lot better run than the church. But Jesus is the Christ appearing among us to reveal God's love, and the church is his people called together to make his presence visible in today's world.

Would we have recognized Jesus as the Christ if we had met him many years ago? Are we able to recognize him today in his body, the church? We are asked to make a leap of faith. If we dare to do it our eyes will be opened and we will see the glory of God.

Bread for the Journey

Being in the Church, Not of It

Often we hear the remark that we have to live *in* the world without being *of* the world. But it may be more difficult to be *in* the church without being *of* the church. Being of the church means being so preoccupied by and involved in the many ecclesial affairs and clerical "ins and outs" that we are no longer focused on Jesus. The church then blinds us to what we came to see and deafens us to what we came to hear. Still, it is *in* the church that Christ dwells, invites us to his table, and speaks to us words of eternal love.

Being *in* the church without being *of* it is a great spiritual challenge.

Bread for the Journey

PART 3

THE DISCIPLINE OF
LIFE TOGETHER

Acknowledging God's Call Today

After seven weeks at the language institute, I am distressed at how superficial the interaction between students and teachers remains. Maybe this is just my own feeling, but I have not experienced an increase in community between the people at the institute. . . .

I experienced it in my own seminary years and saw it at Notre Dame, at the North American College, at Yale Divinity School, and at many other places. Everywhere there was the tendency to live, act, and think as if the real life is not here but there, not now but later. This tendency makes the formation of community so difficult, if not impossible. Community develops where we experience that something significant is taking place *where we are*. It is the fruit of the intimate knowledge that we are together, not because of a common need—such as to learn a language—but because we are called together to help make God's presence visible in the world. Only to the degree that we have this knowledge of God's call can we transcend our own immediate needs and point together to him who is greater than these needs.

I do not know if I will be alive tomorrow, next week, or next year. Therefore today is always more important than tomorrow. We have to be able to say each day, "This is the day the Lord has made, let us rejoice and be glad." If we all would die on the last day of our language training, nobody should have to say, "I wasted my time." The language training itself should have enough inner validity to make its usefulness secondary.

¡Gracias!

God's Joy, Visible in Celebration

The joy of Jesus lifts up life to be celebrated.

Celebration is indeed the word we need here. The divine, ecstatic joy of the house of love becomes manifest in celebration. Celebration marks the life of the disciple of Jesus as well as the life of his new community. The disciple leaves behind the old life in search of a new life. The community is *ec-clesia*, a people "called out" from the land of oppression to the land of freedom. For every disciple as well as for the entire fellowship, following the Lord involves celebration, the ongoing, unceasing lifting up of God's love that has proved itself victorious. Celebration is the concrete way in which God's ecstatic joy becomes visible among us.

It is of great importance to reclaim the word "celebration" as one of the core words of the Christian life. Celebration is not a party on special occasions, but an ongoing awareness that every moment is special and asks to be lifted up and recognized as a blessing from on high. . . .

Celebration lifts up not only the happy moments, but the sad moments as well. Since ecstatic joy embraces *all* of life, it does not shy away from the painful moments of failure, departure, and death. In the house of love even death is celebrated, not because death is desirable or attractive but because in the face of death life can be proclaimed as victorious.

Lifesigns

A Waiting Community

The whole meaning of the Christian community lies in offering each other a space in which we wait for what we have already seen. Christian community is the place where we keep the flame alive among us and take it seriously, so that it can grow and become stronger in us. In this way we can live with courage, trusting that there is a spiritual power in us that allows us to live in this world without being seduced constantly by despair. That is how we dare to say that God is a God of love even when we see hatred all around us. That is why we can claim that God is a God of life even when we see death and destruction and agony all around us. We say it together. We affirm it in each other. Waiting together, nurturing what has already begun, expecting its fulfillment—that is the meaning of marriage, friendship, community, and the Christian life.

The Path of Waiting

Protecting Emptiness for God

The best definition of celibacy, I think, is the definition of Thomas Aquinas. Thomas calls celibacy a vacancy for God. To be a celibate means to be empty for God, to be free and open for his presence, to be available for his service. This view of celibacy, however, has often led to the false idea that being empty for God is a special privilege of celibates, while other people involved in all sorts of interpersonal relationships are not empty but full, occupied as well as preoccupied. If we look at celibacy as a state of life that upholds the importance of God's presence in our lives in contrast with other states of life that lead to entanglement in worldly affairs, we quickly slip into a dangerous elitism considering celibates as domes rising up amid the many low houses of the city.

I think that celibacy can never be considered as a special prerogative of a few members of the people of God. Celibacy, in its deepest sense of creating and protecting emptiness for God, is an essential part of all forms of Christian life: marriage, friendship, single life, and community life. We will never fully understand what it means to be celibate unless we recognize that celibacy is, first of all, an element, and even an essential element in the life of all Christians.

Clowning in Rome

Solitude Strengthens Community

Solitude greeting solitude, that's what community is all about. Community is not the place where we are no longer alone but the place where we respect, protect, and reverently greet one another's aloneness. When we allow our aloneness to lead us into solitude, our solitude will enable us to rejoice in the solitude of others. Our solitude roots us in our own hearts. Instead of making us yearn for company that will offer us immediate satisfaction, solitude makes us claim our center and empowers us to call others to claim theirs. Our various solitudes are like strong, straight pillars that hold up the roof of our communal house. Thus, solitude always strengthens community.

Bread for the Journey

In Solitude We Discover Unity

If we base our life together on our physical proximity, on our ability to spend time together, speak with each other, eat together, and worship together, community life quickly starts fluctuating according to moods, personal attractiveness, and mutual compatibility, and thus will become very demanding and tiring. Solitude is essential for community life because there we begin to discover a unity that is prior to all unifying actions. In solitude we become aware that we were together before we came together and that community life is not a creation of our will but an obedient response to the reality of our being united. Whenever we enter into solitude, we witness to a love that transcends our interpersonal communications and proclaims that we love each other because we have been loved first (1 John 4:19). Solitude keeps us in touch with the sustaining love from which community draws its strength. It sets us free from the compulsions of fear and anger and allows us to be in the midst of an anxious and violent world as a sign of hope and a source of courage. In short, solitude creates that free community that makes bystanders say, "See how they love each other."

Clowning in Rome

Never Taking the World Too Seriously

In solitude we can grow old freely without being preoccupied with our usefulness and we can offer a service which we had not planned on. To the degree that we have lost our dependencies on this world, whatever world means—father, mother, children, career, success or rewards—we can form a community of faith in which there is little to defend but much to share. Because as a community of faith, we take the world seriously but never too seriously. In such a community we can adopt a little of the mentality of Pope John, who could laugh about himself. When some highly decorated official asked him: "Holy Father, how many people work in the Vatican?" he paused a while and then said: "Well, I guess about half of them."

As a community of faith we work hard, but we are not destroyed by the lack of results. And as a community of faith we remind one another constantly that we form a fellowship of the weak, transparent to him who speaks to us in the lonely places of our existence and says: Do not be afraid, you are accepted.

Out of Solitude

Community as a Quality of the Heart

Community, like solitude, is primarily a quality of the heart. While it remains true that we will never know what community is if we never come together in one place, community does not necessarily mean being physically together. We can well live in community while being physically alone. In such a situation, we can act freely, speak honestly, and suffer patiently, because of the intimate bond of love that unites us with others even when time and place separate us from them. The community of love stretches out not only beyond the boundaries of countries and continents but also beyond the boundaries of decades and centuries. Not only the awareness of those who are far away but also the memory of those who lived long ago can lead us into a healing, sustaining, and guiding community. The space for God in community transcends all limits of time and place.

Thus the discipline of community frees us to go wherever the Spirit guides us, even to places we would rather not go. This is the real Pentecost experience. When the Spirit descended on the disciples huddling together in fear, they were set free to move out of their closed room into the world. As long as they were assembled in fear they did not yet form community. But when they had received the Spirit, they became a body of free people who could stay in communion with each other even when they were as far from each other as Rome is from Jerusalem. Thus, when it is the Spirit of God and not fear that unites us in community, no distance of time or place can separate us.

Making All Things New

The Discipline of Community

Community as discipline is the effort to create a free and empty space among people where together we can practice true obedience. Through the discipline of community we prevent ourselves from clinging to each other in fear and loneliness, and clear free space to listen to the liberating voice of God.

It may sound strange to speak of community as discipline, but without discipline community becomes a "soft" word, referring more to a safe, homey, and exclusive place than to the space where new life can be received and brought to its fullness. Wherever true community presents itself, discipline is crucial. It is crucial not only in the many old and new forms of the common life but also in the sustaining relationships of friendship, marriage, and family. To create space for God among us requires the constant recognition of the Spirit of God in each other. When we have come to know the life-giving Spirit of God in the center of our solitude and have thus been able to affirm our true identity, we can also see that same life-giving Spirit speaking to us through our fellow human beings. And when we have come to recognize the life-giving Spirit of God as the source of our life together, we too will more readily hear his voice in our solitude.

Making All Things New

Not a Fearful Clinging

If there is a need for a new morality it is the morality which teaches us the fellowship of the weak as a human possibility. Love then is not a clinging to each other in the fear of an oncoming disaster but an encounter in a freedom that allows for the creation of new life. This love cannot be proved. We can only be invited to it and find it to be true by an engaging response. As long as we experience the Christian life as a life which puts restrictions on our freedom of expression, we have perverted and inverted its essence. The core message of Christianity is exactly this message of the possibility of transcending the taking form of our human existence. The main witness of this message is Jesus who in the exposure of his total vulnerability broke through the chains of death and found his life by losing it. He challenges us to break through the circle of our imprisonment. He challenges us to face our fellow man without fear and to enter with him in the fellowship of the weak, knowing that it will not bring destruction but creation, new energy, new life, and—in the end—a new world.

Intimacy

When All Want the Honor . . .

Adam . . . teaches me the true mystery of community.

Most of my adult life I have tried to show the world that I could do it on my own, that I needed others only to get me back on my lonely road. Those who have helped me helped me to become a strong, independent, self-motivated, creative man who would be able to survive in the long search for individual freedom. With many others, I wanted to become a self-sufficient star. And most of my fellow intellectuals joined me in that desire.

But all of us highly trained individuals are facing today a world on the brink of total destruction. And now we start to wonder how we might join forces to make peace! What kind of peace can this possibly be? Who can paint a portrait of people who all want to take the center seat? Who can build a beautiful church with people who are interested only in erecting the tower? Who can bake a birthday cake with people who want only to put the candles on? You all know the problem. When all want the honor of being the final peacemaker, there never will be peace.

The Path of Peace

Forgiveness, the Cement of Community Life

Community is not possible without the willingness to forgive one another "seventy-seven times" (see Matthew 18:22, NRSV). Forgiveness is the cement of community life. Forgiveness holds us together through good and bad times, and it allows us to grow in mutual love.

But what is there to forgive or to ask forgiveness for? As people who have hearts that long for perfect love, we have to forgive one another for not being able to give or receive that perfect love in our everyday lives. Our many needs constantly interfere with our desire to be there for the other unconditionally. Our love is always limited by spoken or unspoken conditions. What needs to be forgiven? We need to forgive one another for not being God!

Bread for the Journey

Appreciating Other People's Talents

In our competitive world we are so used to thinking in terms of "more" and "less" that we cannot easily see how God can love all human beings with the same unlimited love while at the same time loving each one of them in a totally unique way. Somehow we feel that our election involves another's rejection, that our uniqueness involves another's commonness. Somehow, we think we can only fully enjoy our being loved by God if others are loved less than we are.

But the spiritual life breaks through these distinctions made in the context of rivalry and competition. The spiritual life allows us to experience that the same God who lovingly embraces all people has counted every hair of our heads (see Matthew 10:30), and that the same God who cares for everyone without exception, loves each individual with an exceptional love.

The deeper our prayer becomes the closer we come to this mystery of God's love. And the closer we are to this mystery the better we can live it out in our daily life. It frees us to appreciate other people's talents without feeling diminished by them and to lift up their uniqueness without feeling less unique ourselves. It allows us to celebrate the various ways of being human as a sign of the universal love of God.

Lifesigns

Rejoicing in God's Generosity

Each time I read that parable in which the landowner gives as much to the workers who worked only one hour as to those who did "a heavy day's work in all the heat," a feeling of irritation still wells up inside of me.

Why didn't the landowner pay those who worked many long hours first and then surprise the latecomers with his generosity? Why, instead, does he pay the workers of the eleventh hour first, raising false expectations in the others and creating unnecessary bitterness and jealousy? These questions, I now realize, come from a perspective that is all too willing to impose the economy of the temporal on the unique order of the divine.

It hadn't previously occurred to me that the landowner might have wanted the workers of the early hours to rejoice in his generosity to the latecomers. It never crossed my mind that he might have acted on the supposition that those who had worked in the vineyard the whole day would be deeply grateful to have had the opportunity to do work for their boss, and even more grateful to see what a generous man he is. It requires an interior about-face to accept such a non-comparing way of thinking. But that is God's way of thinking. God looks at his people as children of a family who are happy that those who have done only a little bit are as much loved as those who accomplish much.

The Return of the Prodigal Son

Generosity Creates Family

To become like the Father, I must be as generous as the Father is generous. Just as the Father gives his very self to his children, so must I give my very self to my brothers and sisters. Jesus makes it very clear that it is precisely this giving of self that is the mark of the true disciple. "No one can have greater love than to lay down his life for his friends."

This giving of self is a discipline because it is something that does not come spontaneously. As children of the darkness that rules through fear, self-interest, greed, and power, our great motivators are survival and self-preservation. But as children of the light who know that perfect love casts out all fear, it becomes possible to give away all that we have for others. . . .

Every time I take a step in the direction of generosity, I know that I am moving from fear to love. But these steps, certainly at first, are hard to take because there are so many emotions and feelings that hold me back from freely giving. Why should I give energy, time, money, and yes, even attention to someone who has offended me? . . .

In a spiritual sense, the one who has offended me belongs to my "kin," my "gen." . . . Generosity is a giving that comes from the knowledge of that intimate bond. True generosity is acting on the truth—not on the feeling—that those I am asked to forgive are "kinfolk," and belong to my family. And whenever I act this way, that truth will become more visible to me. Generosity creates the family it believes in.

The Return of the Prodigal Son

True Hospitality

Every good relationship between two or more people, whether it is friendship, marriage, or community, creates space where strangers can enter and become friends. Good relationships are hospitable. When we enter into a home and feel warmly welcomed, we will soon realize that the love among those who live in that home is what makes that welcome possible.

When there is conflict in the home, the guest is soon forced to choose sides. "Are you for him or for her?" "Do you agree with them or with us?" "Do you like him more than you do me?" These questions prevent true hospitality—that is, an opportunity for the stranger to feel safe and discover his or her own gifts. Hospitality is more than an expression of love for the guest. It is also and foremost an expression of love between the hosts.

Bread for the Journey

The Discipline of Listening Together

The discipline of community helps us to be silent together. This disciplined silence is not an embarrassing silence, but a silence in which together we pay attention to the Lord who calls us together. In this way we come to know each other not as people who cling anxiously to our self-constructed identity, but as people who are loved by the same God in a very intimate and unique way.

Here—as with the discipline of solitude—it is often the words of Scripture that can lead us into this communal silence. Faith, as Paul says, comes from hearing. We have to hear the word from each other. When we come together from different geographical, historical, psychological, and religious directions, listening to the same word spoken by different people can create in us a common openness and vulnerability that allow us to recognize that we are safe together in that word. Thus we can come to discover our true identity as a community, thus we can come to experience what it means to be called together, and thus we can recognize that the same Lord whom we discovered in our solitude also speaks in the solitude of our neighbors, whatever their language, denomination, or character. In this listening together to the word of God, a true creative silence can grow. This silence is a silence filled with the caring presence of God. Thus listening together to the word can free us from our competition and rivalry and allow us to recognize our true identity as sons and daughters of the same loving God and brothers and sisters of our Lord Jesus Christ, and thus of each other.

Making All Things New

Words That Create Community

The word is always a word for others. Words need to be heard. When we give words to what we are living, these words need to be received and responded to. A speaker needs a listener. A writer needs a reader.

When the flesh—the lived human experience—becomes word, community can develop. When we say, "Let me tell you what we saw. Come and listen to what we did. Sit down and let me tell you what happened to us. Wait until you hear whom we met," we call people together and make our lives into lives for others. The word brings us together and calls us into community. When the flesh becomes word, our bodies become part of a body of people.

Bread for the Journey

Listening to Each Other

I keep making my mistakes. Tonight I went with Richard and Theresa to *The Stuntman*, a movie about the making of a film. The movie was so filled with images of greed and lust, manipulation and exploitation, fearful and painful sensations, that it filled all the empty spaces that could have been blessed by the spirit of Advent. The film showed me how human beings are willing to waste their money, time, energy, and most precious intellectual and emotional talents to create a product that will fill the eyes and ears of thousands of people with images that can only damage the gentleness that lies dormant in our innermost being and asks to be awakened by a Divine touch.

Why did I go to this spectacle with Richard and Theresa? Richard is a kind Englishman who just returned from years of work with cooperatives in Africa, and Theresa is an Australian woman with great interest in music and handicrafts. Both hope to work together in Latin America and come to know better the beauty of this land and its people.

To be together, why did we need this violent and intrusive film? We could have spent our time so much better listening to each other's stories than watching the stuntman's tricks. Why do we keep missing the most obvious signs of God's coming and allow our hearts to be filled with all those things that keep suggesting, not that the Lord is coming, but that nothing will happen unless we make it happen.

¡Gracias!

Daring to Speak Up

Silence without speaking is as dangerous as solitude without community. They belong together. . . .

It would be tactless, unwise, and even dangerous to expose our innermost being to people who cannot offer us safety and trust. That does not create community; it only causes mutual embarrassment and deepens our shame and guilt. But I do suggest that we need loving and caring friends with whom we can speak from the depth of our heart. Such friends can take away the paralysis that secrecy creates. They can offer us a safe and sacred place, where we can express our deepest sorrows and joys, and they can confront us in love, challenging us to a greater spiritual maturity. We might object by saying: "I do not have such trustworthy friends, and I wouldn't know how to find them." But this objection comes from our fear of drinking the cup that Jesus asks us to drink.

When we are fully committed to the spiritual adventure of drinking our cup to the bottom, we will soon discover that people who are on the same journey will offer themselves to us for encouragement and friendship and love. . . .

When we dare to speak from the depth of our heart to the friends God gives us, we will gradually find new freedom within us and new courage to live our own sorrows and joys to the full. When we truly believe that we have nothing to hide from God, we need to have people around us who represent God for us and to whom we can reveal ourselves with complete trust.

Can You Drink the Cup?

The Disciplines of Trust and Gratitude

The choice of gratitude rarely comes without some real effort. But each time I make it, the next choice is a little easier, a little freer, a little less self-conscious. Because every gift I acknowledge reveals another and another until, finally, even the most normal, obvious, and seemingly mundane event or encounter proves to be filled with grace. There is an Estonian proverb that says: "Who does not thank for little will not thank for much." Acts of gratitude make one grateful because, step by step, they reveal that all is grace.

Both trust and gratitude require the courage to take risks because distrust and resentment, in their need to keep their claim on me, keep warning me how dangerous it is to let go of my careful calculations and guarded predictions. At many points I have to make a leap of faith to let trust and gratitude have a chance: to write a gentle letter to someone who will not forgive me, make a call to someone who has rejected me, speak a word of healing to someone who cannot do the same.

The leap of faith always means loving without expecting to be loved in return, giving without wanting to receive, inviting without hoping to be invited, holding without asking to be held. And every time I make a little leap, I catch a glimpse of the One who runs out to me and invites me into his joy, the joy in which I can find not only myself, but also my brothers and sisters. Thus the disciplines of trust and gratitude reveal the God who searches for me, burning with desire to take away all my resentments and complaints and to let me sit at his side at the heavenly banquet.

The Return of the Prodigal Son

Not All Good Words Are Good for Everyone

It is sad to see that so much pastoral activity is based on the supposition that all the good words are good for everyone. And often the pastor behaves like a poor salesman who wants to sell the whole church as a package at once to everyone he happens to meet.

Much pastoral phoniness is related to the inability to be clinical in pastoral contact and pastoral conversation. Not everyone needs encouragement, not everyone asks for correction, not everyone is ready to be invited to prayer or to hear the name of God. Some ask for silence, some for a single word, some need instruction, some just understanding, some want a smile, some a severe hand, some need support, and some need to be left alone.

Intimacy

Community: The Climate and Support to Sustain Prayer

Prayer as a hopeful and joyful waiting for God is a really unhuman or superhuman task unless we realize that we do not have to wait alone. In the community of faith we can find the climate and the support to sustain and deepen our prayer and we are enabled to constantly look forward beyond our immediate and often narrowing private needs. The community of faith offers the protective boundaries within which we can listen to our deepest longings, not to indulge in morbid introspection, but to find our God to whom they point. In the community of faith we can listen to our feelings of loneliness, to our desires for an embrace or a kiss, to our sexual urges, to our cravings for sympathy, compassion or just a good word; also to our search for insight and to our hope for companionship and friendship. In the community of faith we can listen to all these longings and find the courage, not to avoid them or cover them up, but to confront them in order to discern God's presence in their midst. There we can affirm each other in our waiting and also in the realization that in the center of our waiting the first intimacy with God is found. There we can be patiently together and let the suffering of each day convert our illusions into the prayer of a contrite people. The community of faith is indeed the climate and source of all prayer.

Reaching Out

PART 4

PRAYING WITH
AND FOR OTHERS

The Discipline of Prayer

Unceasing prayer requires the discipline of prayer exercises. Those who do not set aside a certain place and time each day to do nothing else but pray can never expect their unceasing thought to become unceasing prayer. Why is this planned prayer-practice so important? It is important because through this practice God can become fully present to us as a real partner in our conversation.

This discipline of prayer embraces many forms of prayer—communal as well as individual prayer, oral as well as mental prayer. It is of primary importance that we strive for prayer with the understanding that it is an explicit way of being with God. We often say, "All of life should be lived in gratitude," but this is only possible if at certain times we give thanks in a very concrete and visible way. We often say, "All our days should be lived for the glory of God," but this is only possible if a day is regularly set apart to give glory to God. We often say, "We should love one another always," but this is only possible if we regularly perform concrete and unambiguous acts of love. Similarly, it is also true that we can only say, "All our thoughts should be prayer," if there are times in which we make God our only thought.

Common to all disciplined prayer, whether it be liturgical, devotional, or contemplative prayer, is the effort to direct all our attention to God and God alone.

Clowning in Rome

Coming Together around the Promise

One of the most beautiful passages of Scripture is Luke 1:39-56, which tells us about Mary's visit to Elizabeth. What happened when Mary received the words of promise? She went to Elizabeth. Something was happening to Elizabeth as well as to Mary. But how could they live that out?

I find the meeting of these two women very moving, because Elizabeth and Mary came together and enabled each other to wait. Mary's visit made Elizabeth aware of what she was waiting for. The child leapt for joy in her. Mary affirmed Elizabeth's waiting. And then Elizabeth said to Mary, "Blessed is she who believed that the promise made her by the Lord would be fulfilled" (Luke 1:45, JB). And Mary responded, "My soul proclaims the greatness of the Lord" (Luke 1:46, JB). She burst into joy herself. These two women created space for each other to wait. They affirmed for each other that something was happening worth waiting for.

Here we see a model for the Christian community. It is a community of support, celebration, and affirmation in which we can lift up what has already begun in us. The visit of Elizabeth and Mary is one of the Bible's most beautiful expressions of what it means to form community, to be together, gathered around a promise, affirming what is happening among us.

That is what prayer is all about. It is coming together around the promise.

The Path of Waiting

Calling Together the People of God

It is quite understandable that in our large anonymous cities we look for people on our "wave length" to form small communities. Prayer groups, Bible-study clubs and house-churches all are ways of restoring or deepening our awareness of belonging to the people of God. But sometimes a false type of like-mindedness can narrow our sense of community. We all should have the mind of Jesus Christ, but we do not all have to have the mind of a school teacher, a carpenter, a bank director, a congressman or whatever socioeconomic or political group. There is a great wisdom hidden in the old bell tower calling people with very different backgrounds away from their homes to form one body in Jesus Christ. It is precisely by transcending the many individual differences that we can become witnesses of God who allows his light to shine upon poor and rich, healthy and sick alike. But it is also in this encounter on the way to God that we become aware of our neighbor's needs and begin to heal each other's wounds.

Reaching Out

The Language of Christian Community

Prayer is the language of the Christian community. In prayer the nature of the community becomes visible because in prayer we direct ourselves to the one who forms the community. We do not pray to each other, but together we pray to God, who calls us and makes us into a new people. Praying is not one of the many things the community does. Rather, it is its very being. Many discussions about prayer do not take this very seriously. Sometimes it seems as if the Christian community is "so busy" with its projects and plans that there is neither the time nor the mood to pray. But when prayer is no longer its primary concern, and when its many activities are no longer seen and experienced as part of prayer itself, the community quickly degenerates into a club with a common cause but no common vocation.

By prayer, community is created as well as expressed. Prayer is first of all the realization of God's presence in the midst of his people and, therefore, the realization of the community itself. Most clear and most noticeable are the words, the gestures and the silence through which the community is formed. When we listen to the word, we not only receive insight into God's saving work, but we also experience a new mutual bond. When we stand around the altar, eat bread and drink wine, kneel in meditation, or walk in procession we not only remember God's work in human history, but we also become aware of his creative presence here and now. When we sit together in silent prayer, we create a space where we sense that the one we are waiting for is already touching us, as he touched Elijah standing in front of the cave (1 Kings 19:13).

Reaching Out

Community and Individual Prayer Belong Together

Prayer as the language of the community is like our mother tongue. Just as a child learns to speak from his parents, brothers, sisters and friends but still develops his own unique way of expressing himself, so also our individual prayer life develops by the care of the praying community. Sometimes it is hard to point to any specific organizational structure which we can call "our community." Our community is often a very intangible reality made up of people, living as well as dead, present as well as absent, close as well as distant, old as well as young. But without some form of community individual prayer cannot be born or developed. Communal and individual prayer belong together as two folded hands. Without community, individual prayer easily degenerates into egocentric and eccentric behavior, but without individual prayer, the prayer of the community quickly becomes a meaningless routine. Individual and community prayer cannot be separated without harm. This explains why spiritual leaders tend to be very critical of those who want to isolate themselves and why they stress the importance of continuing ties with a larger community where individual prayer can be guided. This also explains why the same leaders have always encouraged the individual member of their communities to spend time and energy in personal prayer, realizing as they do that community alone can never fulfill the desire for the most unique intimate relationship between a human being and his or her God.

Reaching Out

Creating a Home Together

Many human relationships are like the interlocking fingers of two hands. Our loneliness makes us cling to one another, and this mutual clinging makes us suffer immensely because it does not take our loneliness away. But the harder we try, the more desperate we become. Many of these "interlocking" relationships fall apart because they become suffocating and oppressive. Human relationships are meant to be like two hands folded together. They can move away from each other while still touching with the fingertips. They can create space between themselves, a little tent, a home, a safe place to be.

True relationships among people point to God. They are like prayers in the world. Sometimes the hands that pray are fully touching, sometimes there is distance between them. They always move to and from each other, but they never lose touch. They keep praying to the One who brought them together.

Bread for the Journey

Praying Together, Becoming Present to Each Other

Praying together . . . does not mean worrying together, but becoming present for each other in a very real way. Then it becomes possible to share ideas because they are really ours, to communicate feelings because they are actually there, to talk about concerns because they hurt us and we feel their pains in our own soul. Then the formulation of intentions is much more than an at-random choice from the many possible problems we can think of. It becomes, rather, an attempt to be visible and available to each other just as we are at this very moment. What we then ask from each other is not, first of all, to solve a problem or to give a hand, but to affirm each other in the many different ways we experience life. When this takes place, community starts to form and becomes a reality that can be celebrated as an affirmation of the multiformity of being in which we all take part.

Creative Ministry

The Prayers We Said Together, a Safe Place

As we found ourselves gathered around mother's [death] bed, our prayer was easy, free, spontaneous and natural. It offered us words of greater power and meaning than any of the words we could have said to one another. It gave us a sense of unity which could not be created by speculations on the nature of mother's illness or her chances of recovery. It provided a sense of togetherness that was more given than made, and it created a place in which we could rest together.

Some of the prayers we said were ones that mother had taught us as children, prayers that now came to mind again after years of absence. Some were prayers which had never been spoken before, while others were prayers which have been repeated over the centuries by men and women in pain and agony.

The prayers we said together became the place where we could be together without fear or apprehension. They became like a safe house in which we could dwell, communicating things to each other without having to grope for inadequate, self-made expressions. The psalms, the Our Father, the Hail Mary, the Creed, the Litany of the Saints and many other prayers formed the walls of this new house, a safe structure in which we felt free to move closer to each other and to mother, who needed our prayers in her lonely struggle.

In Memoriam

Sabbatical Candles: Praying a Silent Prayer

During my farewell celebration at the Dayspring [community], two large blue candles were presented to me, one for me to take on my journey, and one to go from house to house in the community. They are prayer candles and are meant to remind me and those who sent me of our commitment to each other.

I realize how often my candle is burning! When I write my candle is lit to help make my writing a way of praying, and when I pray the candle is lit to connect me with my friends at home.

Community is so much more than living and working together. It is a bond of the heart that has no physical limitations. Indeed it is candles burning in different places of the world, all praying the same silent prayer of friendship and love.

Sabbatical Journey

"I Will Pray for You"

When we say to people, "I will pray for you," we make a very important commitment. The sad thing is that this remark often remains nothing but a well-meant expression of concern. But when we learn to descend with our mind into our heart, then all those who have become part of our lives are led into the healing presence of God and touched by him in the center of our being. We are speaking here about a mystery for which words are inadequate. It is the mystery that the heart, which is the center of our being, is transformed by God into his own heart, a heart large enough to embrace the entire universe. Through prayer we can carry in our heart all human pain and sorrow, all conflicts and agonies, all torture and war, all hunger, loneliness, and misery, not because of some great psychological or emotional capacity, but because God's heart has become one with ours.

Here we catch sight of the meaning of Jesus' words, "Shoulder my yoke and learn from me, for I am gentle and humble in heart, and you will find rest for your souls. Yes, my yoke is easy and my burden light" (Matthew 11:29-30, JB). Jesus invites us to accept his burden, which is the burden of the whole world, a burden that includes human suffering in all times and places. But this divine burden is light, and we can carry it when our heart has been transformed into the gentle and humble heart of our Lord.

The Way of the Heart

In Praying for Others, I Become the Other

Often I have said to people, "I will pray for you" but how often did I really enter into the full reality of what that means? I now see how indeed I can enter deeply into the other and pray to God from his center. When I really bring my friends and the many I pray for into my innermost being and feel their pains, their struggles, their cries in my own soul, then I leave myself, so to speak, and become them, then I have compassion. Compassion lies at the heart of our prayer for our fellow human beings. When I pray for the world, I become the world; when I pray for the endless needs of the millions, my soul expands and wants to embrace them all and bring them into the presence of God. But in the midst of that experience I realize that compassion is not mine but God's gift to me. I cannot embrace the world, but God can. I cannot pray, but God can pray in me. When God became as we are, that is, when God allowed all of us to enter into his intimate life, it became possible for us to share in his infinite compassion.

In praying for others, I lose myself and become the other, only to be found by the divine love which holds the whole of humanity in a compassionate embrace.

The Genesee Diary

To Pray for Others Requires Gentleness of Heart

Today I imagined my inner self as a place crowded with pins and needles. How could I receive anyone in my prayer when there is no real place for them to be free and relaxed? When I am still so full of preoccupations, jealousies, angry feelings, anyone who enters will get hurt. I had a very vivid realization that I must create some free space in my innermost self so that I may indeed invite others to enter and be healed. To pray for others means to offer others a hospitable place where I can really listen to their needs and pains. Compassion, therefore, calls for a self-scrutiny that can lead to inner gentleness.

If I could have a gentle "interiority"—a heart of flesh and not of stone, a room with some spots on which one might walk barefooted—then God and my fellow humans could meet each other there. Then the center of my heart can become the place where God can hear the prayer for my neighbors and embrace them with his love.

The Genesee Diary

Much of Prayer Is Grieving

It might sound strange to consider grief a way to compassion. But it is. Grief asks me to allow the sins of the world—my own included—to pierce my heart and make me shed tears, many tears, for them. There is no compassion without many tears. If they can't be tears that stream from my eyes, they have to be at least tears that well up from my heart. When I consider the immense waywardness of God's children, . . . and when I look at them through the eyes of God's heart, I cannot but weep and cry out in grief:

Look, my soul, at the way one human being tries to inflict as much pain on another as possible; look at these people plotting to bring harm to their fellows; look at these parents molesting their children; look at this landowner exploiting his workers; look at the violated women, the misused men, the abandoned children. Look, my soul, at the world; see the concentration camps, the prisons, the nursing homes, the hospitals, and hear the cries of the poor.

This grieving is praying. There are so few mourners left in this world. But grief is the discipline of the heart that sees the sin of the world, and knows itself to be the sorrowful price of freedom without which love cannot bloom. I am beginning to see that much of praying is grieving. This grief is so deep not just because the human sin is so great, but also—and more so—because the divine love is so boundless. To become like the Father whose only authority is compassion, I have to shed countless tears and so prepare my heart to receive anyone, whatever their journey has been, and forgive them from that heart.

The Return of the Prodigal Son

Thank God That We Are His Creation

In one of Jesus' stories a Pharisee, standing by himself, prays to God: "God, I thank you that I am not like other people" (Luke 18:11, NRSV).

That's a prayer we often pray. "I'm glad I'm not like him, her, or them. I am lucky not to belong to that family, that country, or that race. I am blessed not to be part of that company, that team, or that crowd!" Most of this prayer is unceasing! Somewhere we are always comparing ourselves with others, trying to convince ourselves that we are better off than they are. It is a prayer that wells up from our fearful selves and guides many of our thoughts and actions.

But this is a very dangerous prayer. It leads from compassion to competition, from competition to rivalry, from rivalry to violence, from violence to war, from war to destruction. It is a prayer that lies all the time, because we are not the difference we try so hard to find. No, our deepest identity is rooted where we are like other people—weak, broken, sinful, but sons and daughters of God.

I even think that we should not thank God for not being like other creatures, animals, plants, or rocks! We should thank God that indeed we are like them, not better or worse but integral parts of God's creation. This is what humility is all about. We belong to the humus, the soil, and it is in this belonging that we can find the deepest reason for gratitude. Our prayer must be, "Thank you, God, that I am worthy to be part of your creation. Be merciful to me a sinner."

Sabbatical Journey

Diary on a Dull Day: Praying in Solidarity

Not much to report today except for many little frustrations, interruptions, and distractions. One of those days that pass without having felt like a real day. Many letters, telephone calls, short visits, little talks, but no real work, no sense of moving, no sense of direction. A day that is so fragmented that it does not seem to come together at all—except perhaps by writing about it!

One of the great gifts of the spiritual life is to know that even days like this are not a total waste. There was still an hour of prayer. There was still the Eucharist, there were still moments of gratitude for the gifts of life. And there is the opportunity to realize that a day like this unites me with thousands, even millions, of people for whom many days are like this, yet who are in no position to do anything about it. So many men, women, and children dream about creative lives; yet because they are not free to shape their own lives, they cannot realize their dreams. I had better pray for them tonight.

The Road to Daybreak

At Lourdes: A Prayer for the Future

Last night I sat in front of the grotto holding a large candle in my hands. It would take more than a day for the candle to burn down, but I wanted to be, for a while, with the flame that would pray all through the night. I prayed for all the people who surround me close by, as well as for those far away. As I looked at the statue of Mary in the niche above the grotto, I lifted up to her not only all those who are part of my family, my community, my circle of friends, but all the people whose lives will go through so many changes in the coming decade. Ten years from now the world will be so different. How will it look? Will there be peace? Will there be less hunger and starvation, less persecution and torture, less homelessness and AIDS? Will there be more unity, more love, more faith? I have no answers to these questions. I know nothing of the future. I don't have to. But I pray for all the people who will journey with me over the next decade and ask Mary to keep them all close to her son.

Jesus and Mary

A Prayer for Those Who Witness

Dear Lord, . . . most people experience this time as an apocalyptic time full of dangers and threats. The chance of a nuclear war is real, hunger is increasing in many parts of the world, violence and hatred cover the front pages of the daily newspapers, and millions of people wonder how they are going to make it through another year, week, or even day.

I pray tonight for all who witness for you in this world: ministers, priests, and bishops, men and women who have dedicated their lives to you, and all those who try to bring the light of the Gospel into the darkness of this age. Give them courage, strength, perseverance, and hope; fill their hearts and minds with the knowledge of your presence, and let them experience your name as their refuge from all dangers. Most of all, give them the joy of your Spirit, so that wherever they go and whomever they meet they will remove the veil of depression, fatalism, and defeatism and will bring new life to the many who live in constant fear of death. Lord, be with all who bring the Good News. Amen.

A Cry for Mercy

PART 5

THE STRENGTH WE GIVE
ONE ANOTHER

Holy Places Where Grace Can Grow

The story of the Visitation teaches me the meaning of friendship and community. How can I ever let God's grace fully work in my life unless I live in a community of people who can affirm it, deepen it, and strengthen it? We cannot live this new life alone. God does not want to isolate us by his grace. On the contrary, he wants us to form new friendships and a new community—holy places where his grace can grow to fullness and bear fruit.

So often new life appears in the church because of an encounter. Dorothy Day never claimed *The Catholic Worker* as her own invention. She always spoke of it as the fruit of her encounter with Peter Maurin. Jean Vanier never claims that he started L'Arche on his own. He always points to his encounter with Père Thomas Philippe as the true beginning of L'Arche. In such encounters two or more people are able to affirm each other in their gifts and encourage each other to "let it happen to them." In this way, new hope is given to the world.

Elizabeth helped Mary to become the Mother of God. Mary helped Elizabeth to become the mother of her Son's prophet, John the Baptist. God may choose us individually, but he always wants us to come together to allow his choice to come to maturity.

The Road to Daybreak

A Fellowship of the Weak

Too often we think or say: "I don't want to bother my friends with my problems. They have enough problems themselves." But the truth is that we honor our friends by entrusting our struggles to them. Don't we ourselves say to our friends who have hidden their feelings of fear and shame from us: "Why didn't you tell me, why did you keep it secret so long?" Obviously, not everyone can receive our hidden pains. But I believe that if we truly desire to grow in spiritual maturity, God will send us the friends we need.

So much of our suffering arises not just out of our painful condition, but from our feeling of isolation in the midst of our pain. Many people who suffer immensely from addiction—be it addiction to alcohol, drugs, sex, or food—find their first real relief when they can share their pain with others and discover that they are truly heard. The many twelve-step programs are a powerful witness to the truth that sharing our pain is the beginning of healing. Here we can see how close sorrow and joy can be. When I discover that I am no longer alone in my struggle and when I start experiencing a new "fellowship in weakness," then true joy can erupt, right in the middle of my sorrow.

Here and Now

In Shared Pain, Hospitality Becomes Community

A shared pain is no longer paralyzing but mobilizing, when understood as a way to liberation. When we become aware that we do not have to escape our pains, but that we can mobilize them into a common search for life, those very pains are transformed from expressions of despair into signs of hope.

Through this common search, hospitality becomes community. Hospitality becomes community as it creates a unity based on the shared confession of our basic brokenness and on a shared hope. This hope in turn leads us far beyond the boundaries of human togetherness to him who calls his people away from the land of slavery to the land of freedom. It belongs to the central insight of the Judaeo-Christian tradition, that it is the call of God which forms the people of God.

A Christian community is therefore a healing community not because wounds are cured and pains are alleviated, but because wounds and pains become openings or occasions for a new vision. Mutual confession then becomes a mutual deepening of hope, and sharing weakness becomes a reminder to one and all of the coming strength.

The Wounded Healer

The Cure for Hypocrisy

This morning at the Eucharist we spoke about hypocrisy, an attitude that Jesus criticizes. I realize that institutional life leads to hypocrisy, because we who offer spiritual leadership often find ourselves not living what we are preaching or teaching. It is not easy to avoid hypocrisy completely because, wanting to speak in the Name of God, the church, or the larger community, we find ourselves saying things larger than ourselves. I often call people to a life that I am not fully able to live myself.

I am learning that the best cure for hypocrisy is community. When as a spiritual leader I live close to those I care for, and when I can be criticized in a loving way by my own people and be forgiven for my own shortcomings, then I won't be considered a hypocrite.

Hypocrisy is not so much the result of not living what I preach but much more of not confessing my inability to fully live up to my own words. I need to become a priest who asks forgiveness of my people for my mistakes.

Sabbatical Journey

The First Step toward Chastity

Often we think about sexuality as a private affair. Sexual fantasies, sexual thoughts, sexual actions are mostly seen as belonging to the private life of a person. But the distinction between the private and the public sphere of life is a false distinction and has created many of the problems we are struggling with in our day. . . .

The first step toward chastity rests in knowing that my sexuality is personal *and* communal. I have to dare to realize that I can harm my neighbors not just by what I do or say, but also by what I think. Confession means sharing my inner mental struggles with a trustworthy human being who can receive that confession in the name of the community. This confession can take place in the context of the sacrament of penance, but it does not have to. What is important is that I start becoming accountable to the community for my inner life. This accountability will gradually take away the obsessive and compulsive quality of sexual thoughts and fantasies. The more I give up my private life and convert it into a personal life for which I am responsible to the community, the easier it will become to live a chaste life—because the community formed and kept together by Jesus will transform my selfish desires into a desire to serve the people of God with every part of my being. Once I have confessed my inner life, the community can let the love of Jesus unmask my false desires, expel the demons, and lead me into the light so that, as a child of light, I can witness to the risen Lord.

The Road to Daybreak

Spiritual Guidance

Word and silence both need guidance. How do we know that we are not deluding ourselves, that we are not selecting those words that best fit our passions, that we are not just listening to the voice of our own imagination? Many have quoted the Scriptures and many have heard voices and seen visions in silence, but only a few have found their way to God. Who can be the judge in his own case? Who can determine if his feelings and insights are leading him in the right direction? Our God is greater than our own heart and mind, and too easily we are tempted to make our heart's desires and our mind's speculations into the will of God. Therefore, we need a guide, a director, a counselor who helps us to distinguish between the voice of God and all the other voices coming from our own confusion or from dark powers far beyond our control. We need someone who encourages us when we are tempted to give it all up, to forget it all, to just walk away in despair. We need someone who discourages us when we move too rashly in unclear directions or hurry proudly to a nebulous goal. We need someone who can suggest to us when to read and when to be silent, which words to reflect upon and what to do when silence creates much fear and little peace.

Reaching Out

Two by Two

Jesus sends the twelve out in pairs (Mark 6:7). We keep forgetting that we are being sent out two by two. We cannot bring good news on our own. We are called to proclaim the Gospel together, in community. There is a divine wisdom here . . . (see Matthew 18:19-20). You might already have discovered for yourself how radically different traveling alone is from traveling together. I have found over and over again how hard it is to be truly faithful to Jesus when I am alone. I need my brothers and sisters to pray with me, to speak with me about the spiritual task at hand, and to challenge me to stay pure in mind, heart, and body. But far more importantly, it is Jesus who heals, not I; Jesus who speaks words of truth, not I; Jesus who is Lord, not I. This is very clearly made visible when we proclaim the redeeming power of God together. Indeed, whenever we minister together, it is easier for people to recognize that we do not come in our own name, but in the name of the Lord Jesus who sent us.

In the past I traveled a lot, preaching and giving retreats as well as commencement and keynote addresses. But I always went alone. Now, however, every time I am sent by the community to speak somewhere, the community tries to send me with a companion.

In the Name of Jesus

Being Angels for Each Other

Joys are hidden in sorrows! I know this from my own times of depression. I know it from living with people with mental handicaps. I know it from looking into the eyes of patients, and from being with the poorest of the poor. We keep forgetting this truth and become overwhelmed by our own darkness. We easily lose sight of our joys and speak of our sorrows as the only reality there is.

We need to remind each other that the cup of sorrow is also the cup of joy, that precisely what causes us sadness can become the fertile ground for gladness. Indeed, we need to be angels for each other, to give each other strength and consolation. Because only when we fully realize that the cup of life is not only a cup of sorrow but also a cup of joy will we be able to drink it.

Can You Drink the Cup?

Carried by Our Brothers and Sisters

Today: feast of St. Thomas the Apostle. During a dialogue homily, two of the monks remarked in different ways that although Thomas did not believe in the resurrection of the Lord, he kept faithful to the community of the apostles. In that community the Lord appeared to him and strengthened his faith. I find this a very profound and consoling thought. In times of doubt or unbelief, the community can "carry you along," so to speak; it can even offer on your behalf what you yourself overlook, and can be the context in which you may recognize the Lord again.

John Eudes remarked that Dydimus, the name of Thomas, means "twin," as the Gospel says, and that the fathers had commented that all of us are "two people," a doubting one and a believing one. We need the support and love of our brothers and sisters to prevent our doubting person from becoming dominant and destroying our capacity for belief.

The Genesee Diary

Choosing a Milieu to Grow in the Spirit

It is very hard to live a life of prayer in a milieu where no one prays or speaks lovingly about prayer. It is nearly impossible to deepen our communion with God when those with whom we live and work reject or even ridicule the idea that there is a loving God. It is a superhuman task to keep setting our hearts on the kingdom when all those whom we know and talk with are setting their hearts on everything but the kingdom.

It is not surprising that people who live in a secular milieu—where God's name is never mentioned, prayer unknown, the Bible never read, and conversation about the life in the Spirit completely absent—cannot sustain their communion with God for very long. I have discovered how sensitive I am to the milieu in which I live. With my community, words about God's presence in our life come spontaneously and with great ease. However, when I join in a business meeting in downtown Toronto or keep company with those who work with AIDS patients, a conversation about God often creates embarrassment or even anger and generally ends up in a debate about the pros and cons of religion that leaves everybody unhappy.

When we are serious about living a spiritual life we are responsible for the milieu where it can grow and mature. Although we might not be able to create the ideal context for a life in the Spirit, we have many more options than we often claim for ourselves.

Here and Now

A Good Letter Can Change a Day

One of the experiences of silence is that many people, good old friends and good old enemies, start seeking attention. Often a thought led to a prayer and a prayer to a letter and a letter to a real feeling of peace and warmth. A few times, after having dropped a small pile of letters in the mailbox, I had a deep sense of joy, of reconciliation, of friendship. When I was able to express gratitude to those who had given me much, sorrow to those whom I had offended, recognition to those I had forgotten, or sympathy to those who are in grief, my heart seemed to grow and a weight fell from me. These letters seemed to restore the part of me wounded by past resentment and take away the obstacles that prevented me from bringing my history into my present prayer.

But there also is another side. Perhaps part of my letter writing shows that I do not want to be forgotten here, that I hope that there still are people "out there" who think of me. Maybe part of my letter writing is my newly found way of seducing people into paying attention to me here in the enclosure of a monastery. I am sure that that is part of it because just as I feel happy when I drop my letters in the mailbox, so do I feel disappointed when I don't receive much in return. . . .

Meanwhile, it remains remarkable how little is said and written about letter writing as an important form of ministry. A good letter can change the day for someone in pain, can chase away feelings of resentment, can create a smile and bring joy to the heart.

The Genesee Diary

We Need Mary to Find Our Way to Joy

Mary creates a space for us where we can become children as Jesus became a child. . . .

How much I want to say to you, as Jesus said: "Become like children" (see Matthew 18:3, NRSV). Many of us have become so serious and intense, so filled with preoccupations about the future of the world and the church, so burdened by our own loneliness and isolation, that our hearts are veiled by a dark sadness, preventing us from exuding the peace and the joy of God's children. You know as well as I that when our words are full of warnings, our eyes full of fears, our bodies full of unfulfilled needs and our actions full of distrust, we cannot expect ever to create around us a community that shines as a light in the darkness.

When Jesus said to his beloved disciple: "Behold, your mother" (John 19:27, RSV), he gave Mary to us. He wants us to have a mother who can guide us toward our true childhood, not the childhood of an infant that does not yet know its own wounds, but the childhood of the disciple who has come to see that, underneath all his personal woundedness, there is a first love untainted by the ambiguities and ambivalences of human affection. We need Mary to find our way to the joy and peace of the children of God.

Jesus and Mary

The Hidden Promise

When our good plans are interrupted by poor weather, our well-organized careers by illness or bad luck, our peace of mind by inner turmoil, our hope for peace by a new war, our desire for a stable government by a constant changing of the guards, and our desire for immortality by real death, we are tempted to give in to a paralyzing boredom or to strike back in destructive bitterness. But when we believe that patience can make our expectations grow, then fate can be converted into a vocation, wounds into a call for deeper understanding, and sadness into a birthplace of joy.

I would like to tell you the story of a middle-aged man whose career was suddenly interrupted by the discovery of leukemia, a fatal blood cancer. All his life plans crumbled and all his ways had to change. But slowly he was able to ask himself no longer: "Why did this happen to me? What did I do wrong to deserve this fate?" but instead: "What is the promise hidden in this event?" When his rebellion became a new quest, he felt that he could give strength and hope to other cancer patients and, that by facing his condition directly, he could make his pain into a source of healing for others. To this day, this man not only does more for patients than many ministers are able to do, but he also refound his life on a level that he had never known before.

Out of Solitude

God Will Provide the Friends We Need

To whom do we go for advice? With whom do we spend our free evenings? With whom are we going on vacation? Sometimes we speak or act as if we have little choice in the matter. Sometimes we act as though we will be lucky if there is anyone who wants to be our friend. But that is a very passive and even fatalistic attitude. If we truly believe that God loves us with an unlimited, unconditional love, then we can trust that there are women and men in this world who are eager to show us that love. But we cannot wait passively until someone shows up to offer us friendship. As people who trust in God's love, we must have the courage and the confidence to say to someone through whom God's love becomes visible to us: "I would like to get to know you. I would like to spend time with you. I would like to develop a friendship with you. What about you?"

There will be no's, there will be the pain of rejection. But when we determine to avoid all no's and all rejections, we will never create the milieu where we can grow stronger and deepen in love. God became human for us to make divine love tangible. That is what incarnation is all about. That incarnation not only happened long ago, but it continues to happen for those who trust that God will give us the friends we need. But the choice is ours!

Here and Now

A Deep Desire to Bless Others

Claiming your own blessedness always leads to a deep desire to bless others. The characteristic of the blessed ones is that, wherever they go, they always speak words of blessing. It is remarkable how easy it is to bless others, to speak good things to and about them, to call forth their beauty and truth, when you yourself are in touch with your own blessedness. The blessed one always blesses. And people want to be blessed! This is so apparent wherever you go. No one is brought to life through curses, gossip, accusations or blaming. There is so much of that taking place around us all the time. And it calls forth only darkness, destruction and death. As the "blessed ones," we can walk through this world and offer blessings. It doesn't require much effort. It flows naturally from our hearts. When we hear within ourselves the voice calling us by name and blessing us, the darkness no longer distracts us. The voice that calls us the Beloved will give us words to bless others and reveal to them that they are no less blessed than we.

Life of the Beloved

To Give Someone a Blessing . . .

Let me first tell you what I mean by the word "blessing." In Latin, to bless is *benedicere*. The word "benediction" that is used in many churches means literally: speaking (*dictio*) well (*bene*) or saying good things of someone. That speaks to me. I need to hear good things said of me, and I know how much you have the same need. Nowadays, we often say: "We have to affirm each other." Without affirmation, it is hard to live well. To give someone a blessing is the most significant affirmation we can offer. It is more than a word of praise or appreciation; it is more than pointing out someone's talents or good deeds; it is more than putting someone in the light. To give a blessing is to affirm, to say "yes" to a person's Belovedness. And more than that: to give a blessing creates the reality of which it speaks. There is a lot of mutual admiration in this world, just as there is a lot of mutual condemnation. A blessing goes beyond the distinction between admiration or condemnation, between virtues or vices, between good deeds or evil deeds. A blessing touches the original goodness of the other and calls forth his or her Belovedness. . . .

The blessings that we give to each other are expressions of the blessing that rests on us from all eternity. It is the deepest affirmation of our true self. It is not enough to be chosen. We also need an ongoing blessing that allows us to hear in an ever-new way that we belong to a loving God who will never leave us alone, but will remind us always that we are guided by love on every step of our lives.

Life of the Beloved

A Unique Opportunity in Death

What I learned about dying is that I am called to die for others. The very simple truth is that the way in which I die affects many people. If I die with much anger and bitterness, I will leave my family and friends behind in confusion, guilt, shame, or weakness. When I felt my death approaching, I suddenly realized how much I could influence the hearts of those whom I would leave behind. If I could truly say that I was grateful for what I had lived, eager to forgive and be forgiven, full of hope that those who loved me would continue their lives in joy and peace, and confident that Jesus who calls me would guide all who somehow had belonged to my life—if I could do that—I would, in the hour of my death, reveal more true spiritual freedom than I had been able to reveal during all the years of my life. I realized on a very deep level that dying is the most important act of living. It involves a choice to bind others with guilt or to set them free with gratitude. This choice is a choice between a death that gives life and a death that kills. I know that many people live with the deep feeling that they have not done for those who have died what they wanted to do, and have no idea how to be healed from that lingering feeling of guilt. The dying have the unique opportunity to set free those whom they leave behind.

Beyond the Mirror

Easter: An Event for the Friends of Jesus

After the Gospel we spoke together about the resurrection. Liz, who works with many anguished people, said, "We have to keep rolling away the large stones that prevent people from coming out of their graves." Elizabeth . . . said, "After the resurrection Jesus had breakfast again with his friends and showed them the importance of the small, ordinary things of life." Sue . . . said, "It is such a comfort to know that Jesus' wounds remain visible in his risen body. Our wounds are not taken away, but become sources of hope to others."

As everyone spoke, I felt very close to the Easter event. It was not a spectacular event forcing people to believe. Rather, it was an event for the friends of Jesus, for those who had known him, listened to him, and believed in him. It was a very intimate event: a word here, a gesture there, and a gradual awareness that something new was being born—small, hardly noticed, but with the potential to change the face of the earth. Mary of Magdala heard her name. John and Peter saw the empty grave. Jesus' friends felt their hearts burn in encounters that find expression in the remarkable words "He is risen." All had remained the same, while all had changed.

The five of us . . . knew deep in our hearts that for us too all had changed, while all had remained the same. Our struggles are not ended. On Easter morning we can still feel the pains of the world, the pains of our family and friends, the pains of our hearts. They are still there and will be there for a long time. Still, all is different because we have met Jesus and he has spoken to us.

The Road to Daybreak

PART 6

THE GIFTS WE DISCOVER
IN ONE ANOTHER

When Care Is Our First Concern

Care is something other than cure. *Cure* means "change." A doctor, a lawyer, a minister, a social worker—they all want to use their professional skills to bring about changes in people's lives. They get paid for whatever kind of cure they can bring about. But cure, desirable as it may be, can easily become violent, manipulative, and even destructive if it does not grow out of care. Care is being with, crying out with, suffering with, feeling with. Care is compassion. It is claiming the truth that the other person is my brother or sister, human, mortal, vulnerable, like I am.

When care is our first concern, cure can be received as a gift. Often we are not able to cure, but we are always able to care. To care is to be human.

Bread for the Journey

The Fruits of the Spirit as Gifts

The more we touch the intimate love of God which creates, sustains, and guides us, the more we recognize the multitude of fruits that come forth from that love. They are fruits of the Spirit, such as: joy, peace, kindness, goodness, and gentleness. When we encounter any of these fruits, we always experience them as gifts.

When, for instance, we enjoy a good atmosphere in the family, a peaceful mood among friends, or a spirit of cooperation and mutual support in the community, we intuitively know that we did not produce it. It cannot be made, imitated, or exported. To people who are jealous, and who would like to have our joy and peace, we cannot give a formula to produce it or a method to acquire it. It is always perceived as a gift, to which the only appropriate response is gratitude.

Every time we experience real goodness or gentleness we know it is a gift. If we say: "Well, she gets paid to be nice to us," or "He only says such friendly things because he wants something from us," we can no longer receive that goodness as a gift. We grow from receiving and giving gifts.

Lifesigns

Gifts Are More Important than Talents

More important than our talents are our gifts. We may have only a few talents, but we have many gifts. Our gifts are the many ways in which we express our humanity. They are part of who we are: friendship, kindness, patience, joy, peace, forgiveness, gentleness, love, hope, trust and many others. These are the true gifts we have to offer each other.

Somehow I have known this for a long time, especially through my personal experience of the enormous healing power of these gifts. But since my coming to live in a community with mentally handicapped people, I have rediscovered this simple truth. Few, if any, of those people have talents they can boast of. Few are able to make contributions to our society that allow them to earn money, compete on the open market or win awards. But how splendid are their gifts! Bill, who suffered intensely as a result of shattered family relationships, has a gift for friendship that I have seldom experienced. Even when I grow impatient or distracted by other people, he remains always faithful and continues to support me in all I do. Linda, who has a speech handicap, has a unique gift for welcoming people. Many who have stayed in our community remember Linda as the one who made them feel at home. Adam, who is unable to speak, walk or eat without help and who needs constant support, has the great gift of bringing peace to those who care for him and live with him. The longer I live in L'Arche, the more I recognize the true gifts that in us, seemingly nonhandicapped people, often remain buried.

Life of the Beloved

Receiving the Gifts of the Poor

After a few weeks among the poor in Lima, Peru, I was so impressed by their gifts of joy, peace, and gentleness—notwithstanding their great needs—that I came to realize that my vocation was as much that of receiver as of giver. Perhaps it was more important for me to receive from the poor the many gifts born of their love than to try to make myself valuable in their eyes.

For us, however, it is far from easy to be receiving people. We so need to take on useful projects, change inefficient ways, and solve burning problems, that a deep change of heart and mind is required of us to become receivers. Somehow it seems hard for us to truly believe that God loves the people of Central and South America as much as he loves us, and that his love is as fruitful there as anywhere else.

When we come to a clear understanding that we are all brothers and sisters in the house of God—whatever our race, religion, or nationality—we realize that in God there is no distinction between haves and have-nots. We all have gifts to offer and a need to receive. I am increasingly convinced that one of the greatest missionary tasks is to receive the fruits of the lives of the poor, the oppressed, and the suffering as gifts offered for the salvation of the rich.

Lifesigns

Children: Gifts to a Community

Many parents question the value of baptism of newborn babies. But one important aspect of early baptism is that when the parents bring their child to the church, they are reminded that the child is not their own private property but a gift of God given to a community that is much larger than the immediate family. In our culture it seems that all the responsibility for the child rests on the biological parents. The high-rise apartment buildings, in which families live in their small isolated units and are often fearful of their neighbors, do indeed not offer the small child much more to depend on than his own parents.

During a visit in Mexico, sitting on a bench in one of the village plazas, I saw how much larger the family of the children was. They were hugged, kissed and carried around by aunts, uncles, friends and neighbors, and it seemed that the whole community spending its evening playfully in the plaza became father and mother for the little ones. Their affection, and their fearless movements made me aware that for them everyone was family.

The church is perhaps one of the few places left where we can meet people who are different than we are but with whom we can form a larger family. Taking our children out of the house and bringing them to the church for baptism is at least an important reminder of the larger community in which they are born and which can offer them a free space to grow to maturity without fear.

Reaching Out

Entering into the Children's Joy

The children always challenge me to live in the present. They want me to be with them here and now, and they find it hard to understand that I might have other things to do or to think about. After all my experiences with psychotherapy, I suddenly have discovered the great healing power of children. Every time Pablito, Johnny, and Maria run up to welcome me, pick up my suitcase, and bring me to my "roof-room," I marvel at their ability to be fully present to me. Their uninhibited expression of affection and their willingness to receive it pull me directly into the moment and invite me to celebrate life where it is found. Whereas in the past coming home meant time to study, to write letters, and to prepare for classes, it now first of all means time to play.

In the beginning, I had to get used to finding a little boy under my bed, a little girl in my closet, and a teenager under my table, but now I am disappointed when I find my friends asleep at night. I did not know what to expect when I came to Pamplona Alta. I wondered how the poverty, the lack of good food and good housing would affect me; I was afraid of becoming depressed by the misery I would see. But God showed me something else first: affectionate, open, and playful children who are telling me about love and life in ways no book was ever able to do. I now realize that only when I can enter with the children into their joy will I be able to enter also with them into their poverty and pain. God obviously wants me to walk into the world of suffering with a little child on each hand.

¡Gracias!

Eyes to Discover Joy

My life at Daybreak [community] has given me eyes to discover joy where many others see only sorrow. Talking with a homeless man on a Toronto street doesn't feel so frightening anymore. Soon money is not the main issue. It becomes: "Where are you from? Who are your friends? What is happening in your life?" Eyes meet, hands touch, and there is—yes, often completely unexpected—a smile, a burst of laughter, and a true moment of joy. The sorrow is still there, but something has changed by my no longer standing in front of others but sitting with them and sharing a moment of togetherness.

And the immense suffering of the world? How can there be joy among the dying, the hungry, the prostitutes, the refugees and the prisoners? How does anyone dare to speak about joy in the face of the unspeakable human sorrows surrounding us?

And yet, it is there! For anyone who has the courage to enter our human sorrows deeply, there is a revelation of joy, hidden like a precious stone in the wall of a dark cave.

Can You Drink the Cup?

Celebrating Birthdays

Birthdays need to be celebrated. I think it is more important to celebrate a birthday than a successful exam, a promotion, or a victory. Because to celebrate a birthday means to say to someone: "Thank you for being you." Celebrating a birthday is exalting life and being glad for it. On a birthday we do not say: "Thanks for what you did, or said, or accomplished." No, we say: "Thank you for being born and being among us."

On birthdays we celebrate the present. We do not complain about what happened or speculate about what will happen, but we lift someone up and let everyone say: "We love you."

I know a friend who, on his birthday, is picked up by his friends, carried to the bathroom, and thrown clothes and all into a tub full of water. Everyone eagerly awaits his birthday, even he himself. I have no idea where this tradition came from, but to be lifted up and "re-baptized" seems like a very good way to have your life celebrated. We are made aware that although we have to keep our feet on the ground, we are created to reach to the heavens, and that, although we easily get dirty, we can always be washed clean again and our life given a new start.

Celebrating a birthday reminds us of the goodness of life, and in this spirit we really need to celebrate people's birthdays every day, by showing gratitude, kindness, forgiveness, gentleness, and affection. These are ways of saying: "It's good that you are alive; it's good that you are walking with me on this earth. Let's be glad and rejoice. This is the day that God has made for us to be and to be together."

Here and Now

At Table Together

Isn't a meal together the most beautiful expression of our desire to be given to each other in our brokenness? The table, the food, the drinks, the words, the stories: are they not the most intimate ways in which we not only express the desire to give our lives to each other, but also to do this in actuality? I very much like the expression "breaking bread together," because there the breaking and the giving are so clearly one. When we eat together we are vulnerable to one another. Around the table we can't wear weapons of any sort. Eating from the same bread and drinking from the same cup call us to live in unity and peace. This becomes very visible when there is a conflict. Then, eating and drinking together can become a truly threatening event, then the meal can become the most dreaded moment of the day. We all know about painful silences during dinner. They contrast starkly with the intimacy of eating and drinking together, and the distance between those sitting around the table can be unbearable.

On the other hand, a really peaceful and joyful meal together belongs to the greatest moments of life.

Don't you think that our desire to eat together is an expression of our even deeper desire to be food for one another? Don't we sometimes say: "That was a very nurturing conversation. That was a refreshing time"? I think that our deepest human desire is to give ourselves to each other as a source of physical, emotional and spiritual growth.

Life of the Beloved

Great Gifts of Healing for Each Other

A very intense day. Many people came by for the Sacrament of Reconciliation or just to talk about their pains and fears. As I listened to their feelings of loneliness, rejection, guilt, and shame, I became overwhelmed by the sense of isolation we human beings can feel. While our sufferings are so similar and our struggles so much a part of our shared humanity, we often live as if we are the only ones who experience the pain that paralyzes us! At one point during the day I felt a desire to bring together all those who had spoken to me this day. I wanted to ask them to share their stories with one another so that they could discover how much they had in common and in this way become a source of consolation and comfort to each other.

Why do we keep hiding our deepest feelings from each other? We suffer much, but we also have great gifts of healing for each other. The mystery is that by hiding our pain we also hide our ability to heal. Even in such a loving and caring community as this, there is more loneliness than necessary. We are called to confess to each other and forgive each other, and thus to discover the abundant mercy of God. But at the same time, we are so terribly afraid of being hurt more than we already are. This fear keeps us prisoners, even when the prison has no walls! I see better every day how radical Jesus' message of love really is.

The Road to Daybreak

In Receiving I Reveal the Gift

When Jesus was carrying the cross to Golgotha, the soldiers came across a man from Cyrene, called Simon, and they enlisted him to carry the cross because it had become too heavy for Jesus alone. He was unable to carry it to the place of his execution and needed the help of a stranger to fulfill his mission. So much weakness, so much vulnerability. Jesus needs us to fulfill his mission. He needs people to carry the cross with him and for him. He came to us to show us the way to his Father's home. He came to offer us a new dwelling place, to give us a new sense of belonging, to point us to the true safety. But he cannot do it alone. The hard, painful work of salvation is a work in which God becomes dependent on human beings. Yes, God is full of power, glory, and majesty. But God chose to be among us as one of us—as a dependent human being. . . .

Every time I am willing to break out of my false need for self-sufficiency and dare to ask for help, a new community emerges—a fellowship of the weak—strong in the trust that together we can be a people of hope for a broken world. Simon of Cyrene discovered a new communion. Everyone whom I allow to touch me in my weakness and help me to be faithful to my journey to God's home will come to realize that he or she has a gift to offer that may have remained hidden for a very long time. To receive help, support, guidance, affection, and care may well be a greater call than that of giving these things because in receiving I reveal the gift to the givers and a new life together can begin.

Walk with Jesus

The Gift of Self-Confrontation

Sometimes a life of compassion offers a gift you are not so eager to receive: the gift of self-confrontation. . . .

I remember quite vividly one such moment of self-confrontation. During a lecture trip to Texas, I had bought a large cowboy hat for Raymond, one of the handicapped members of the house in which I lived. I looked forward to coming home and giving him my gift.

But when Raymond, whose needs for attention and affirmation were as boundless as my own, saw my gift he started yelling at me: "I don't need your silly gift. I have enough gifts. I have no place for them in my room. My walls are already full. You better keep your gift. I don't need it." His words opened a deep wound in me. He made me realize that I *wanted* to be his friend, but instead of spending time with him and offering him my attention, I had given him an expensive gift. Raymond's angry response to the Texan hat confronted me with my inability to enter into a personal relationship with him and develop a real friendship. The hat, instead of being seen as an expression of friendship, was seen as a substitute for it.

Obviously, all of this didn't happen consciously on my side or on Raymond's side. But when Raymond's outburst brought me to tears I realized that my tears were, most of all, tears about my own inner brokenness.

This self-confrontation too is a gift of the compassionate life. It is a gift very hard to receive, but a gift that can teach us much and help us in our own search for wholeness and holiness.

Here and Now

The Gift of Silence

I remember an experience of feeling totally abandoned—my heart in anguish, my mind going crazy with despair, my body shaking wildly. I cried, screamed, and pounded the floors and the walls. Two friends were with me. They didn't say anything. They just were there. When, after several hours, I calmed down a little bit, they were still there. They put their arms around me and held me, rocking me like a little child. Then we simply sat on the floor. My friends gave me something to drink; I couldn't speak. There was silence . . . safe silence.

Today I think of that experience as a turning point in my life. I don't know how I would have survived without my friends.

I also remember the time that a friend came to me and told me that his wife had left him that day. He sat in front of me, tears streaming from his eyes. I didn't know what to say. There simply was nothing to say. My friend didn't need words. What he needed was simply to be with a friend. I held his hands in mine, and we sat there . . . silently. For a moment, I wanted to ask him how and why it all had happened, but I knew that this was not the time for questions. It was the time just to be together as friends who have nothing to say, but are not afraid to remain silent together.

Here and Now

The Gift of Peace

O Lord Jesus . . . whenever I touch the hearts of your broken people, I touch your heart. Your broken heart and the broken heart of the world are one.

O Lord, it is true. I know it. Every time I overcame the fear of my own wounds and the wounds of those around me and dared to touch them gently, joy and peace came to me in ways I never dreamed of. Sometimes it was just sitting in silence and letting my loneliness be; sometimes it was just listening to a stranger who revealed his anguish to me; sometimes it was waiting with a lonely woman until death set her free; sometimes it was looking in silence at a Rembrandt painting with a friend; sometimes it was crying many tears while holding on to someone who was not afraid of me. O Lord, so often did I wander away to safe places—high, powerful, prestigious and quite visible. But often I felt a strange isolation there as though people around me had become puppets and you a distant stranger. But every time I chose again to turn back to your heart, my own heart started to burn, and an undefinable peace came to me, a peace emerging from the wounds I touched.

Heart Speaks to Heart

The Gift of Gratitude

In many of the families I visited nothing was certain, nothing predictable, nothing totally safe. Maybe there would be food tomorrow, maybe there would be work tomorrow, maybe there would be peace tomorrow. Maybe, maybe not. But whatever is given—money, food, work, a handshake, smile, a good word, or an embrace—is a reason to rejoice and say *gracias*. What I claim as a right, my friends in Bolivia and Peru received as a gift; what is obvious to me was a joyful surprise to them; what I take for granted, they celebrate in thanksgiving; what for me goes by unnoticed became for them a new occasion to say thanks.

And slowly I learned. I learned what I must have forgotten somewhere in my busy, well-planned, and very "useful" life. I learned that everything that is, is freely given by the God of love. All is grace. Light and water, shelter and food, work and free time, children, parents and grandparents, birth and death—it is all given to us. Why? So that we can say *gracias*, thanks: thanks to God, thanks to each other, thanks to all and everyone.

More than anything else, I learned to say thanks. The familiar expression "let us say grace" now means something very different than saying a few prayers before a meal. It now means lifting up the whole of life into the presence of God and all his people in gratitude.

¡Gracias!

Solidarity in Grief

Daniel, a handicapped man, had just learned that his father had died. It requires special care and attention to offer consolation and support to people who express themselves with so much difficulty. . . . He spoke with difficulty about his grandmother, whose grief over her son's death had touched him deeply. People listened to him with much attention and love. Then Daniel made a surprising proposal. He invited all the members of the foyer to come to his room and pray. This was remarkable since Daniel never joined in evening prayer and was very protective of his privacy. People never just went into his room. But tonight he invited everyone to enter more deeply into his life to be with him in his grief. He placed some candles and small statues on the floor. Pépé, one of the other handicapped men, brought a picture of his deceased mother and put it next to the candles and the statues. I was deeply moved by this gesture of solidarity in grief. Pépé had little to say, but by putting his own mother's photograph on the floor of Daniel's room, he said more than any of us could with our sympathetic words.

The twelve of us huddled together in Daniel's small bedroom and prayed for him, his father, his mother, his grandmother, and his friends. We showed him a picture of Jesus and asked him who it was. "It is Jesus, the hidden one," he answered. For Daniel, Jesus was hard to reach, but tonight this small group of friends made Jesus more tangible than ever before.

The Road to Daybreak

PART 7

A NEW COMMUNION WITH THOSE WITH THOSE WHO HAVE DIED

Prayer for Full Liberation

Throughout Latin America, All Souls Day is a special feast, the day in which people pay tribute to and enter into communion with those who have died. The place where this celebration of the lasting bonds with the dead can be experienced is the cemetery.

For me, the day started quietly. I spent an hour in the early morning in silent prayer for my mother and all the family members and friends who had died over the last years. From that intimate center, I let the eyes of my mind wander into wider and wider circles. I first saw the many acquaintances in my own little world who are no longer with me, then I thought about the many whose deaths I had learned of through newspapers, radio, and television, and finally I saw the thousands and thousands who had lost their lives through hunger and violence and whose names would always remain unknown to me. Suddenly, I found myself surrounded by a crowd of people who had been cruelly snatched away from life without a prayer, a word of consolation, or even a kiss on the forehead. To all of these I was intimately linked—so intimately that their total freedom had come to depend more and more on this ongoing connection stretching out far beyond the boundary of death. Indeed, part of the meaning of life for the living is our opportunity to pray for the full liberation of those who died before us.

¡Gracias!

A Protective Cloud Covering Me

Gradually I am becoming aware of a new dimension in my prayer life. It is hard to find words for it, but it feels like a protective presence of God, Mary, the angels, and the saints that exists in the midst of distractions, fears, temptations, and inner confusion.

While my prayers were not at all intensive or profound, I had a real desire to spend time in prayer this week. I enjoyed just sitting in the small dark side chapel of the mother house of the Vincentian Sisters. I felt surrounded by goodness, gentleness, kindness, and acceptance. I felt as if angels' wings were keeping me safe: a protective cloud covering me and keeping me there. Though it is very hard to express, this new experience is the experience of being protected against the dangers of a seductive world. But this protection is very soft, gentle, caring. Not the protection of a wall or a metal screen. It is more like a hand on my shoulder or a kiss on my forehead. But for all this protection, I am not taken away from the dangers. I am not lifted from the seductive world. I am not removed from violence, hatred, lust, and greed. In fact, I feel them in the center of my being, screaming for my full attention. They are restless and noisy. Still, this hand, these lips, these eyes are present and I know that I am safe, held in love, cared for, and protected by the good spirits of heaven.

So I am praying while not knowing how to pray. I am resting while feeling restless, at peace while tempted, safe while still anxious, surrounded by a cloud of light while still in darkness, in love while still doubting.

The Road to Daybreak

Saints: Powerful Guides on the Way to God

Here saints are like roommates with whom you can have long conversations. . . .

I remember from my high school years with the Jesuits and from my seminary years, how the secular and the sacred cycles always intersected each other. But here there is nothing to intersect with. Here the only cycle is the liturgical cycle, and here the time is indeed redeemed. You see and feel that the monastic day, week and year are meant to be time-bound anticipations of a heavenly existence. Already you are invited to participate in the intimate life of the Holy Trinity, Father, Son, and Spirit, and to be joyful because of those who came so close to God in their historical existence that they have a special place in the heavenly kingdom. . . .

In the past, the saints had very much moved to the background of my consciousness. During the last few months, they re-entered my awareness as powerful guides on the way to God. I read the lives of many saints and great spiritual men and women, and it seems that they have become real members of my spiritual family, always present to offer suggestions, ideas, advice, consolation, courage, and strength. It is very hard to keep your heart and mind directed toward God when there are no examples to help you in your struggle. Without saints you easily settle for less-inspiring people and quickly follow the ways of others who for a while seem exciting but who are not able to offer lasting support. I am happy to have been able to restore my relationship with many great saintly men and women in history who, by their lives and works, can be real counselors to me.

The Genesee Diary

The Long Journey of the People of God

Franz and Robert Johna drove Jonas and me to Strasbourg. At 11 A.M. we participated in the Eucharistic celebration in the cathedral. . . .

After the Gospel reading of the transfiguration, the Franciscan climbed the richly carved pulpit in the middle of the cathedral. All the worshipers turned their chairs around so that they could see him and listen attentively. He spoke about the transfiguration not only of Jesus, but of all creation. As he spoke he pointed to the brilliant yellow, white, and blue rose window above the cathedral entrance. He said, "Though this is a great piece of art, we can only see its full splendor when the sun shines through it." Then he explained how our bodies, the work of our hands, and all that exists can shine with splendor only when we let God's light shine through them. As he spoke, I kept looking at the magnificent rose window—at thirteen meters across, the largest ever made—and I had a new sense of the transfiguration that took place on Mount Tabor: God's light bursting forth from the body of Jesus. Six centuries ago a rose-window was made that today helps me to see the glory of Christ in a new way. Again I felt part of the long journey of the people of God through the centuries. There was much that was old and much that was new. There were statues of saints, kings, and queens of long ago. There were also friendly priests in dungarees and turtlenecks, women acolytes, and many cars parked around the cathedral. I could see history moving. But again and again there recurred that same story on the second Sunday of Lent, the story of the transfiguration of Jesus.

The Road to Daybreak

A Fisherman's Feast Day

Dear Lord, your disciple James longed for a special place in your kingdom, a place close to you. You had a special affection for him; you took him with you when you entered the house of Jairus to heal his daughter and when you went up to Mount Tabor to pray. But you made it clear that friendship with you includes suffering with you. When you asked him if he could drink the cup of suffering, he said yes with the same ambition with which he desired a special place in your kingdom.

You loved this young, zealous man whose main desire was to be with you at all times and in all places. You told him and all your disciples that service, not power, was the standard in your kingdom, and slowly you changed his heart from one set on influence into one searching for the deepest place. He responded, followed you, and drank the same cup you drank. He became one of the first apostles to die for you.

O Lord, convert my heart as you converted the heart of your disciple James. Amen.

A Cry for Mercy

Spiritual Wisdom Passed Down Through the Centuries

The spiritual wisdom of many Christians, who in the course of history have dedicated their lives to prayer, is preserved and relived in the different traditions, lifestyles or spiritualities that remain visible in contemporary Christianity. In fact, our first and most influential guides are often the prayer customs, styles of worship and modes of speaking about God that pervade our different milieux. Each spiritual milieu has its own emphasis. Here silence is stressed, there study of the Scriptures; here individual meditation is central, there communal worship; here poverty is the unifying concept, there it is obedience; here the great mystical experiences are suggested as the way to perfection, there the little way of common daily life. Much of the emphasis depends on the time in which a new spirituality found its beginning, on the personal character of the man or woman who was or is its main inspiration and on the particular needs to which it responds.

The fact that these spiritualities are mostly related to influential historical personalities with great visibility helps us to use them as real guides in the search for our own personal way. . . .

I remember meeting one day a very shy, somewhat withdrawn man. Although he was very intelligent, it seemed as if the world was just too big for him. Any suggestion that he do something outstanding or special scared him. For him, the little way, the conscientious living of the small realities of everyday life was the way of prayer. When he spoke about the little Thérèse of Lisieux, his spiritual guide, his eyes lit up and he looked full of joy. But his more passionate neighbor needed the example of Anthony of the Desert or Bernard of Clairvaux and other great spiritual athletes to help him in his search for an authentic spiritual life.

Without such inspiring guides, it is very difficult to remain faithful to the desire to find our own way. It is a hard and often lonely search and we constantly need new insights, support and comfort to persevere. The really great saints of history don't ask for imitation. Their way was unique and cannot be repeated. But they invite us into their lives and offer a hospitable space for our own search. Some turn us off and make us feel uneasy; others even irritate us, but among the many great spiritual men and women in history we may find a few, or maybe just one or two, who speak the language of our heart and give us courage. These are our guides. Not to be imitated but to help us live our lives just as authentically as they lived theirs. When we have found such guides we have good reason to be grateful and even better reasons to listen attentively to what they have to say.

Reaching Out

When Death Is Affirmed, Hope Finds Roots

I still see vividly the simple funeral of a Donegal farmer. The priest and a few men carried the humble coffin to the cemetery. After the coffin was put in the grave, the men filled the grave with sand and covered it again with the patches of grass which had been laid aside. Two men stamped with their boots on the sod so that it was hardly possible to know that this was a grave. Then one of the men took two pieces of wood, bound them together in the form of a cross and stuck it in the ground. Everyone made a quick sign of the cross and left silently. No words, no solemnity, no decoration. Nothing of that. But it never has been made so clear to me that someone was dead, not asleep but dead, not passed away but dead, not laid to rest but dead, plain dead. When I saw those two men stamping on the ground in which they had buried their friend, I knew that for these farmers of Donegal there were no funeral-home games to play. But their realism became a transcendent realism by the simple unadorned wooden cross saying that where death is affirmed, hope finds its roots. "Unless a wheat grain falls on the ground and dies, it remains only a single grain; but if it dies, it yields a rich harvest" (John 12:24, JB).

The Mass we celebrated for Kevin's mother was simple and beautiful. Kevin came afterward to shake hands with the celebrant and concelebrants. All the way through the ceremony I saw the simple men of Donegal digging their grave and sticking their cross in the ground. "Margaret, may she dwell in the house of the Lord . . . "

The Genesee Diary

Those Who Have Gone Before Us

The way people relate to their own past is of crucial importance for their life experience. The past can become a prison in which you feel you are caught forever, or a constant reason to compliment yourself. Your past can make you deeply ashamed or guilt-ridden, but it can also be the cause of pride and self-content. Some people will say with remorse: "If I could live my life again, I certainly would do it differently"; others will say with self-assertion: "You might think I am an old, weak man, but look at those trophies there; I won those when I was young." Memory is one of the greatest sources of human happiness and human suffering. If we want to celebrate our lives in the present, we cannot cut off ourselves from our past. We are instead invited to look at our history as the sequence of events that brought us where we are now and that help us to understand what it means to be here at this moment in this world.

He who celebrates life will not make his past a prison nor a source of pride, but will face the facts of history and fully accept them as the elements that allow him to claim his experience as his own.

When we commemorate during a liturgical celebration those who have gone before us, we do much more than direct a pious thought to our deceased family and friends; we recognize that we stand in the midst of history and that the affirmation of our present condition is grounded in the recognition that we were brought to where we are now by the innumerable people who lived *their* lives before we were given the chance to live *ours*.

Creative Ministry

Closer to Me than Ever

Questions became very real to me in those confusing weeks after mother's death. I said to myself, "This is a time of waiting for the Spirit of truth to come, and woe unto me if, by forgetting her, I prevent her from doing God's work in me." I sensed that something much more than a filial act of remembering was at stake, much more than an honoring of my dead mother, much more than a holding on to her beautiful example. Very specifically, what was at stake was the life of the Spirit in me. To remember her does not mean telling her story over and over again to my friends, nor does it mean pictures on the wall or a stone on her grave; it does not even mean constantly thinking about her. No. It means making her a participant in God's ongoing work of redemption by allowing her to dispel in me a little more of my darkness and lead me a little closer to the light. In these weeks of mourning she died in me more and more every day, making it impossible for me to cling to her as my mother. Yet by letting her go I did not lose her. Rather, I found that she is closer to me than ever. In and through the Spirit of Christ, she indeed is becoming a part of my very being.

In Memoriam

When Our Spirits Are Completely Revealed

As the Beloved, I am called to trust that life is a preparation for death as a final act of giving. Not only are we called to live for others, but also to die for others. How is this possible?

Let me tell you first about three dear friends who have died during the past few months: David Osler, Murray McDonnell and Pauline Vanier. I miss them. Their deaths are a painful loss. Whenever I think of them, I feel the biting pain that they are no longer in their homes with their families and friends. I can no longer call them, visit them, hear their voices or see their faces. I feel immense grief. But I believe deeply that their deaths are more than a loss. Their deaths are also a gift.

The deaths of those whom we love and who love us, open up the possibility of a new, more radical communion, a new intimacy, a new belonging to each other. If love is, indeed, stronger than death, then death has the potential to deepen and strengthen the bonds of love. It was only after Jesus had left his disciples that they were able to grasp what he truly meant to them. But isn't that true for all who die in love?

It is only when we have died that our spirits can completely reveal themselves. David, Murray and Pauline were all beautiful people, but they were also people whose ability to love was limited by their many needs and wounds. Now, after their deaths, the needs and wounds that kept their spirits captive no longer inhibit them from giving their full selves to us. Now they can send us their spirits, and we can live in a new communion with them.

Life of the Beloved

Easter: Bridging the Distance

On Easter Sunday I read the Gospel story about Peter and John running to the tomb and finding it empty. There were more than a hundred visitors in the abbey church, some from far away and some from nearby, some young and some old, some formally and some casually dressed. Sitting with forty monks around the huge rock that serves as the altar, they gave me a real sense of the church. After reading the Gospel, I preached. I had seldom preached on Easter Sunday during my twenty-two years of priesthood, and I felt very grateful that I could announce to all who were present: "The Lord is risen; he is risen indeed." Everyone listened with great attention and I had a sense that the risen Christ was really among us, bringing us his peace. During the Eucharist, I prayed for you [father, in Holland], for mother [now deceased], and for all who are dear to us. I felt that the risen Christ brought us all together, bridging not only the distance between Holland and the United States but also that between life and death. Lent was long, sometimes very hard, and not without its dark moments and tempting demons. But now, in the light of the resurrection of Christ, Lent seems to have been short and easy. I guess this is true for all of life. In darkness we doubt that there will ever be light, but in the light we soon forget how much darkness there was.

A Letter of Consolation

PART 8

A WIDER AND DEEPER LOVE

The Community of Your Heart

The more you have loved and have allowed yourself to suffer because of your love, the more you will be able to let your heart grow wider and deeper. When your love is truly giving and receiving, those whom you love will not leave your heart even when they depart from you. They will become part of your self and thus gradually build a community within you.

Those you have deeply loved become part of you. The longer you live, there will always be more people to be loved by you and to become part of your inner community. The wider your inner community becomes, the more easily you will recognize your own brothers and sisters in the strangers around you. Those who are alive within you will recognize those who are alive around you. The wider the community of your heart, the wider the community around you. Thus the pain of rejection, absence, and death can become fruitful. Yes, as you love deeply the ground of your heart will be broken more and more, but you will rejoice in the abundance of the fruit it will bear.

The Inner Voice of Love

Trust That God Will Give You the People

You [Henri] have to start seeing yourself as your truthful friends see you. As long as you remain blind to your own truth, you keep putting yourself down and referring to everyone else as better, holier, and more loved than you are. You look up to everyone in whom you see goodness, beauty, and love because you do not see any of these qualities in yourself. As a result, you begin leaning on others without realizing that you have everything you need to stand on your own feet.

You cannot force things, however. You cannot *make* yourself see what others see. You cannot fully claim yourself when parts of you are still wayward. You have to acknowledge where you are and affirm that place. You have to be willing to live your loneliness, your incompleteness, your lack of total incarnation fearlessly, and trust that God will give you the people to keep showing you the truth of who you are.

The Inner Voice of Love

Remain Anchored

It is important to remain as much in touch as possible with those who know you [Henri], love you, and protect your vocation. If you visit people with great needs and deep struggles that you can easily recognize in your own heart, remain anchored in your home community. Think about your community as holding a long line that girds your waist. Wherever you are, it holds that line. Thus you can be very close to people in need of your healing without losing touch with those who protect your vocation. Your community can pull you back when its members see that you are forgetting why you were sent out.

When you feel a burgeoning need for sympathy, support, affection, and care from those to whom you are being sent, remember that there is a place where you can receive those gifts in a safe and responsible way. Do not let yourself be seduced by the dark powers that imprison those you want to set free. Keep returning to those to whom you belong and who keep you in the light. It is that light that you desire to bring into the darkness. You do not have to fear anyone as long as you remain safely anchored in your community. Then you can carry the light far and wide.

The Inner Voice of Love

A Reflection of a Greater Love

Dear Lord, I bring before you all the people who experience failure in their search for a creative, affectionate relationship. Many single people feel lonely and unable to sustain a friendship for a long period of time; many married people feel frustrated in their marriage and separate to go different ways; many children cannot speak to their parents; and many parents have become afraid of their children. All around me I see the hunger for love and the inability to experience it in a deep and lasting way.

O Lord, look with favor on us, your people, and impart your love to us—not as an idea or concept, but as a lived experience. We can only love each other because you have loved us first. Let us know that first love so that we can see all human love as a reflection of a greater love, a love without conditions and limitations.

Heal those who feel hurt in their most intimate self, who feel rejected, misunderstood, and even misused. Show them your healing love and help them on their way to forgiveness and reconciliation. Amen.

A Cry for Mercy

Let Our Love Be Strong and Fearless

Dear Lord, when your side was pierced, and water and blood came forth, the church was born: a new community founded on baptism and the sacrificial breaking of the bread. It is your love, manifested on the cross, that gave birth to a new life, a new way of living, a new fellowship, a new message.

O Lord, I pray that your church as a community of love born on your cross will withstand the powers that are threatening us with division and destruction. Make the love of your church strong enough to dismantle the nuclear warheads, missiles, and submarines and bring sanity to those who keep making more and more of them day after day. Give your people insight, courage and faith to take a stand against this madness, in which defense becomes the same as mutual annihilation.

O Lord, let our love be strong and fearless, and let your name be spoken as a sign of hope. Amen.

A Cry for Mercy

Acknowledgments

Selections from *Adam* by Henri J. M. Nouwen. Copyright © 1977. Reprinted by permission of Orbis Books.

Selections from *Behold the Beauty of the Lord* by Henri J. M. Nouwen. Copyright © 1987 by Ave Maria Press. Used with permission of the publisher.

Selections from *Beyond the Mirror.* Copyright © 1990 by Henri J. M. Nouwen. Reprinted by permission of the Crossroad Publishing Company.

Selections from *Bread for the Journey: A Daybook of Wisdom and Faith* by Henri J. M. Nouwen. Copyright © 1997 by Henri J. M. Nouwen. Reprinted by permission of HarperCollins Publishers.

Selections from *Can You Drink the Cup?* by Henri J. M. Nouwen. Copyright © 1996 by Ave Maria Press. Used with permission of the publisher.

Selections from *Clowning in Rome* by Henri J. M. Nouwen, copyright © 1979 by Henri J. M. Nouwen. Used by permission of Doubleday, a division of Random House, Inc.

Selections from *Creative Ministry* by Henri J. M. Nouwen, copyright © 1971 by Henri J. M. Nouwen. Used by permission of Doubleday, a division of Random House, Inc.

Selections from *A Cry for Mercy* by Henri J. M. Nouwen, copyright © 1981 by Henri J. M. Nouwen. Used by permission of Doubleday, a division of Random House, Inc.

Selections from *The Genesee Diary* by Henri J. M. Nouwen, copyright © 1976 by Henri J. M. Nouwen. Used by permission of Doubleday, a division of Random House, Inc.